C-1845

CAREER EXAMINATION SERIES

THIS IS YOUR **PASSBOOK®** FOR ...

BUYER I

NLC®
NATIONAL LEARNING CORPORATION®
passbooks.com

COPYRIGHT NOTICE

This book is SOLELY intended for, is sold ONLY to, and its use is RESTRICTED to individual, bona fide applicants or candidates who qualify by virtue of having seriously filed applications for appropriate license, certificate, professional and/or promotional advancement, higher school matriculation, scholarship, or other legitimate requirements of educational and/or governmental authorities.

This book is NOT intended for use, class instruction, tutoring, training, duplication, copying, reprinting, excerption, or adaptation, etc., by:

1) Other publishers
2) Proprietors and/or Instructors of «Coaching» and/or Preparatory Courses
3) Personnel and/or Training Divisions of commercial, industrial, and governmental organizations
4) Schools, colleges, or universities and/or their departments and staffs, including teachers and other personnel
5) Testing Agencies or Bureaus
6) Study groups which seek by the purchase of a single volume to copy and/or duplicate and/or adapt this material for use by the group as a whole without having purchased individual volumes for each of the members of the group
7) Et al.

Such persons would be in violation of appropriate Federal and State statutes.

PROVISION OF LICENSING AGREEMENTS. — Recognized educational, commercial, industrial, and governmental institutions and organizations, and others legitimately engaged in educational pursuits, including training, testing, and measurement activities, may address request for a licensing agreement to the copyright owners, who will determine whether, and under what conditions, including fees and charges, the materials in this book may be used them. In other words, a licensing facility exists for the legitimate use of the material in this book on other than an individual basis. However, it is asseverated and affirmed here that the material in this book CANNOT be used without the receipt of the express permission of such a licensing agreement from the Publishers. Inquiries re licensing should be addressed to the company, attention rights and permissions department.

All rights reserved, including the right of reproduction in whole or in part, in any form or by any means, electronic or mechanical, including photocopying, recording, or by any information storage and retrieval system, without permission in writing from the Publisher.

Copyright © 2020 by

NLC®

National Learning Corporation

212 Michael Drive, Syosset, NY 11791
(516) 921-8888 • www.passbooks.com
E-mail: info@passbooks.com

PUBLISHED IN THE UNITED STATES OF AMERICA

PASSBOOK® SERIES

THE *PASSBOOK® SERIES* has been created to prepare applicants and candidates for the ultimate academic battlefield – the examination room.

At some time in our lives, each and every one of us may be required to take an examination – for validation, matriculation, admission, qualification, registration, certification, or licensure.

Based on the assumption that every applicant or candidate has met the basic formal educational standards, has taken the required number of courses, and read the necessary texts, the *PASSBOOK® SERIES* furnishes the one special preparation which may assure passing with confidence, instead of failing with insecurity. Examination questions – together with answers – are furnished as the basic vehicle for study so that the mysteries of the examination and its compounding difficulties may be eliminated or diminished by a sure method.

This book is meant to help you pass your examination provided that you qualify and are serious in your objective.

The entire field is reviewed through the huge store of content information which is succinctly presented through a provocative and challenging approach – the question-and-answer method.

A climate of success is established by furnishing the correct answers at the end of each test.

You soon learn to recognize types of questions, forms of questions, and patterns of questioning. You may even begin to anticipate expected outcomes.

You perceive that many questions are repeated or adapted so that you can gain acute insights, which may enable you to score many sure points.

You learn how to confront new questions, or types of questions, and to attack them confidently and work out the correct answers.

You note objectives and emphases, and recognize pitfalls and dangers, so that you may make positive educational adjustments.

Moreover, you are kept fully informed in relation to new concepts, methods, practices, and directions in the field.

You discover that you arre actually taking the examination all the time: you are preparing for the examination by "taking" an examination, not by reading extraneous and/or supererogatory textbooks.

In short, this PASSBOOK®, used directedly, should be an important factor in helping you to pass your test.

BUYER I

DUTIES
Performs and assists with technical work in the purchase of assigned types of commodities in connection with the central purchasing operations of the county; performs related work as required.

SCOPE OF THE EXAMINATION
The multiple-choice written test will cover knowledges, skills, and/or abilities in such areas as:
1. **Arithmetic computation with calculator** - These questions test for the ability to use a calculator to do basic computations. Questions will involve addition, subtraction, multiplication and division. You may also be asked to calculate averages, to use percents, and to round an answer to the nearest whole number.
2. **Principles and practices of purchasing** - These questions test for candidates' knowledge of the principles guiding governmental purchasing operations and the ability to put them into practice. These questions may deal with but are not necessarily, limited to such matters as the analysis of bids; the use of specifications, the award of contracts, the analysis of market factors that can affect the cost of a purchase, and the application of a set of rules to determine how to proceed with a purchase. Some arithmetic computation may be necessary. No specific knowledge of purchasing laws, rules and regulations will be required to answer these questions.
3. **Preparing written material** - These questions test for the ability to present information clearly and accurately, and to organize paragraphs logically and comprehensibly. For some questions, you will be given information in two or three sentences followed by four restatements of the information. You must then choose the best version. For other questions, you will be given paragraphs with their sentences out of order. You must then choose, from four suggestions, the best order for the sentences.
4. **Understanding and interpreting written material** - These questions test how well you comprehend written material. You will be provided with brief reading selections and will be asked questions about the selections. All the information required to answer the questions will be presented in the selections; you will not be required to have any special knowledge relating to the subject areas of the selections.

HOW TO TAKE A TEST

I. YOU MUST PASS AN EXAMINATION

A. *WHAT EVERY CANDIDATE SHOULD KNOW*

Examination applicants often ask us for help in preparing for the written test. What can I study in advance? What kinds of questions will be asked? How will the test be given? How will the papers be graded?

As an applicant for a civil service examination, you may be wondering about some of these things. Our purpose here is to suggest effective methods of advance study and to describe civil service examinations.

Your chances for success on this examination can be increased if you know how to prepare. Those "pre-examination jitters" can be reduced if you know what to expect. You can even experience an adventure in good citizenship if you know why civil service exams are given.

B. *WHY ARE CIVIL SERVICE EXAMINATIONS GIVEN?*

Civil service examinations are important to you in two ways. As a citizen, you want public jobs filled by employees who know how to do their work. As a job seeker, you want a fair chance to compete for that job on an equal footing with other candidates. The best-known means of accomplishing this two-fold goal is the competitive examination.

Exams are widely publicized throughout the nation. They may be administered for jobs in federal, state, city, municipal, town or village governments or agencies.

Any citizen may apply, with some limitations, such as the age or residence of applicants. Your experience and education may be reviewed to see whether you meet the requirements for the particular examination. When these requirements exist, they are reasonable and applied consistently to all applicants. Thus, a competitive examination may cause you some uneasiness now, but it is your privilege and safeguard.

C. *HOW ARE CIVIL SERVICE EXAMS DEVELOPED?*

Examinations are carefully written by trained technicians who are specialists in the field known as "psychological measurement," in consultation with recognized authorities in the field of work that the test will cover. These experts recommend the subject matter areas or skills to be tested; only those knowledges or skills important to your success on the job are included. The most reliable books and source materials available are used as references. Together, the experts and technicians judge the difficulty level of the questions.

Test technicians know how to phrase questions so that the problem is clearly stated. Their ethics do not permit "trick" or "catch" questions. Questions may have been tried out on sample groups, or subjected to statistical analysis, to determine their usefulness.

Written tests are often used in combination with performance tests, ratings of training and experience, and oral interviews. All of these measures combine to form the best-known means of finding the right person for the right job.

II. HOW TO PASS THE WRITTEN TEST

A. NATURE OF THE EXAMINATION

To prepare intelligently for civil service examinations, you should know how they differ from school examinations you have taken. In school you were assigned certain definite pages to read or subjects to cover. The examination questions were quite detailed and usually emphasized memory. Civil service exams, on the other hand, try to discover your present ability to perform the duties of a position, plus your potentiality to learn these duties. In other words, a civil service exam attempts to predict how successful you will be. Questions cover such a broad area that they cannot be as minute and detailed as school exam questions.

In the public service similar kinds of work, or positions, are grouped together in one "class." This process is known as *position-classification*. All the positions in a class are paid according to the salary range for that class. One class title covers all of these positions, and they are all tested by the same examination.

B. FOUR BASIC STEPS

1) Study the announcement

How, then, can you know what subjects to study? Our best answer is: "Learn as much as possible about the class of positions for which you've applied." The exam will test the knowledge, skills and abilities needed to do the work.

Your most valuable source of information about the position you want is the official exam announcement. This announcement lists the training and experience qualifications. Check these standards and apply only if you come reasonably close to meeting them.

The brief description of the position in the examination announcement offers some clues to the subjects which will be tested. Think about the job itself. Review the duties in your mind. Can you perform them, or are there some in which you are rusty? Fill in the blank spots in your preparation.

Many jurisdictions preview the written test in the exam announcement by including a section called "Knowledge and Abilities Required," "Scope of the Examination," or some similar heading. Here you will find out specifically what fields will be tested.

2) Review your own background

Once you learn in general what the position is all about, and what you need to know to do the work, ask yourself which subjects you already know fairly well and which need improvement. You may wonder whether to concentrate on improving your strong areas or on building some background in your fields of weakness. When the announcement has specified "some knowledge" or "considerable knowledge," or has used adjectives like "beginning principles of..." or "advanced ... methods," you can get a clue as to the number and difficulty of questions to be asked in any given field. More questions, and hence broader coverage, would be included for those subjects which are more important in the work. Now weigh your strengths and weaknesses against the job requirements and prepare accordingly.

3) Determine the level of the position

Another way to tell how intensively you should prepare is to understand the level of the job for which you are applying. Is it the entering level? In other words, is this the position in which beginners in a field of work are hired? Or is it an intermediate or advanced level? Sometimes this is indicated by such words as "Junior" or "Senior" in the class title. Other jurisdictions use Roman numerals to designate the level – Clerk I, Clerk II, for example. The word "Supervisor" sometimes appears in the title. If the level is not indicated by the title, check the description of duties. Will you be working under very close supervision, or will you have responsibility for independent decisions in this work?

4) Choose appropriate study materials

Now that you know the subjects to be examined and the relative amount of each subject to be covered, you can choose suitable study materials. For beginning level jobs, or even advanced ones, if you have a pronounced weakness in some aspect of your training, read a modern, standard textbook in that field. Be sure it is up to date and has general coverage. Such books are normally available at your library, and the librarian will be glad to help you locate one. For entry-level positions, questions of appropriate difficulty are chosen – neither highly advanced questions, nor those too simple. Such questions require careful thought but not advanced training.

If the position for which you are applying is technical or advanced, you will read more advanced, specialized material. If you are already familiar with the basic principles of your field, elementary textbooks would waste your time. Concentrate on advanced textbooks and technical periodicals. Think through the concepts and review difficult problems in your field.

These are all general sources. You can get more ideas on your own initiative, following these leads. For example, training manuals and publications of the government agency which employs workers in your field can be useful, particularly for technical and professional positions. A letter or visit to the government department involved may result in more specific study suggestions, and certainly will provide you with a more definite idea of the exact nature of the position you are seeking.

III. KINDS OF TESTS

Tests are used for purposes other than measuring knowledge and ability to perform specified duties. For some positions, it is equally important to test ability to make adjustments to new situations or to profit from training. In others, basic mental abilities not dependent on information are essential. Questions which test these things may not appear as pertinent to the duties of the position as those which test for knowledge and information. Yet they are often highly important parts of a fair examination. For very general questions, it is almost impossible to help you direct your study efforts. What we can do is to point out some of the more common of these general abilities needed in public service positions and describe some typical questions.

1) General information

Broad, general information has been found useful for predicting job success in some kinds of work. This is tested in a variety of ways, from vocabulary lists to questions about current events. Basic background in some field of work, such as sociology or economics, may be sampled in a group of questions. Often these are principles which have become familiar to most persons through exposure rather than through formal training. It is difficult to advise you how to study for these questions; being alert to the world around you is our best suggestion.

2) Verbal ability

An example of an ability needed in many positions is verbal or language ability. Verbal ability is, in brief, the ability to use and understand words. Vocabulary and grammar tests are typical measures of this ability. Reading comprehension or paragraph interpretation questions are common in many kinds of civil service tests. You are given a paragraph of written material and asked to find its central meaning.

3) Numerical ability

Number skills can be tested by the familiar arithmetic problem, by checking paired lists of numbers to see which are alike and which are different, or by interpreting charts and graphs. In the latter test, a graph may be printed in the test booklet which you are asked to use as the basis for answering questions.

4) Observation

A popular test for law-enforcement positions is the observation test. A picture is shown to you for several minutes, then taken away. Questions about the picture test your ability to observe both details and larger elements.

5) Following directions

In many positions in the public service, the employee must be able to carry out written instructions dependably and accurately. You may be given a chart with several columns, each column listing a variety of information. The questions require you to carry out directions involving the information given in the chart.

6) Skills and aptitudes

Performance tests effectively measure some manual skills and aptitudes. When the skill is one in which you are trained, such as typing or shorthand, you can practice. These tests are often very much like those given in business school or high school courses. For many of the other skills and aptitudes, however, no short-time preparation can be made. Skills and abilities natural to you or that you have developed throughout your lifetime are being tested.

Many of the general questions just described provide all the data needed to answer the questions and ask you to use your reasoning ability to find the answers. Your best preparation for these tests, as well as for tests of facts and ideas, is to be at your physical and mental best. You, no doubt, have your own methods of getting into an exam-taking mood and keeping "in shape." The next section lists some ideas on this subject.

IV. KINDS OF QUESTIONS

Only rarely is the "essay" question, which you answer in narrative form, used in civil service tests. Civil service tests are usually of the short-answer type. Full instructions for answering these questions will be given to you at the examination. But in case this is your first experience with short-answer questions and separate answer sheets, here is what you need to know:

1) Multiple-choice Questions

Most popular of the short-answer questions is the "multiple choice" or "best answer" question. It can be used, for example, to test for factual knowledge, ability to solve problems or judgment in meeting situations found at work.

A multiple-choice question is normally one of three types—
- It can begin with an incomplete statement followed by several possible endings. You are to find the one ending which *best* completes the statement, although some of the others may not be entirely wrong.
- It can also be a complete statement in the form of a question which is answered by choosing one of the statements listed.
- It can be in the form of a problem – again you select the best answer.

Here is an example of a multiple-choice question with a discussion which should give you some clues as to the method for choosing the right answer:

When an employee has a complaint about his assignment, the action which will *best* help him overcome his difficulty is to
    A. discuss his difficulty with his coworkers
    B. take the problem to the head of the organization
    C. take the problem to the person who gave him the assignment
    D. say nothing to anyone about his complaint

In answering this question, you should study each of the choices to find which is best. Consider choice "A" – Certainly an employee may discuss his complaint with fellow employees, but no change or improvement can result, and the complaint remains unresolved. Choice "B" is a poor choice since the head of the organization probably does not know what assignment you have been given, and taking your problem to him is known as "going over the head" of the supervisor. The supervisor, or person who made the assignment, is the person who can clarify it or correct any injustice. Choice "C" is, therefore, correct. To say nothing, as in choice "D," is unwise. Supervisors have and interest in knowing the problems employees are facing, and the employee is seeking a solution to his problem.

2) True/False Questions

The "true/false" or "right/wrong" form of question is sometimes used. Here a complete statement is given. Your job is to decide whether the statement is right or wrong.

SAMPLE: A roaming cell-phone call to a nearby city costs less than a non-roaming call to a distant city.

This statement is wrong, or false, since roaming calls are more expensive.
This is not a complete list of all possible question forms, although most of the others are variations of these common types. You will always get complete directions for

answering questions. Be sure you understand *how* to mark your answers – ask questions until you do.

V. RECORDING YOUR ANSWERS

Computer terminals are used more and more today for many different kinds of exams.

For an examination with very few applicants, you may be told to record your answers in the test booklet itself. Separate answer sheets are much more common. If this separate answer sheet is to be scored by machine – and this is often the case – it is highly important that you mark your answers correctly in order to get credit.

An electronic scoring machine is often used in civil service offices because of the speed with which papers can be scored. Machine-scored answer sheets must be marked with a pencil, which will be given to you. This pencil has a high graphite content which responds to the electronic scoring machine. As a matter of fact, stray dots may register as answers, so do not let your pencil rest on the answer sheet while you are pondering the correct answer. Also, if your pencil lead breaks or is otherwise defective, ask for another.

Since the answer sheet will be dropped in a slot in the scoring machine, be careful not to bend the corners or get the paper crumpled.

The answer sheet normally has five vertical columns of numbers, with 30 numbers to a column. These numbers correspond to the question numbers in your test booklet. After each number, going across the page are four or five pairs of dotted lines. These short dotted lines have small letters or numbers above them. The first two pairs may also have a "T" or "F" above the letters. This indicates that the first two pairs only are to be used if the questions are of the true-false type. If the questions are multiple choice, disregard the "T" and "F" and pay attention only to the small letters or numbers.

Answer your questions in the manner of the sample that follows:

32. The largest city in the United States is
   A. Washington, D.C.
   B. New York City
   C. Chicago
   D. Detroit
   E. San Francisco

1) Choose the answer you think is best. (New York City is the largest, so "B" is correct.)
2) Find the row of dotted lines numbered the same as the question you are answering. (Find row number 32)
3) Find the pair of dotted lines corresponding to the answer. (Find the pair of lines under the mark "B.")
4) Make a solid black mark between the dotted lines.

VI. BEFORE THE TEST

Common sense will help you find procedures to follow to get ready for an examination. Too many of us, however, overlook these sensible measures. Indeed, nervousness and fatigue have been found to be the most serious reasons why applicants fail to do their best on civil service tests. Here is a list of reminders:

- Begin your preparation early – Don't wait until the last minute to go scurrying around for books and materials or to find out what the position is all about.
- Prepare continuously – An hour a night for a week is better than an all-night cram session. This has been definitely established. What is more, a night a week for a month will return better dividends than crowding your study into a shorter period of time.
- Locate the place of the exam – You have been sent a notice telling you when and where to report for the examination. If the location is in a different town or otherwise unfamiliar to you, it would be well to inquire the best route and learn something about the building.
- Relax the night before the test – Allow your mind to rest. Do not study at all that night. Plan some mild recreation or diversion; then go to bed early and get a good night's sleep.
- Get up early enough to make a leisurely trip to the place for the test – This way unforeseen events, traffic snarls, unfamiliar buildings, etc. will not upset you.
- Dress comfortably – A written test is not a fashion show. You will be known by number and not by name, so wear something comfortable.
- Leave excess paraphernalia at home – Shopping bags and odd bundles will get in your way. You need bring only the items mentioned in the official notice you received; usually everything you need is provided. Do not bring reference books to the exam. They will only confuse those last minutes and be taken away from you when in the test room.
- Arrive somewhat ahead of time – If because of transportation schedules you must get there very early, bring a newspaper or magazine to take your mind off yourself while waiting.
- Locate the examination room – When you have found the proper room, you will be directed to the seat or part of the room where you will sit. Sometimes you are given a sheet of instructions to read while you are waiting. Do not fill out any forms until you are told to do so; just read them and be prepared.
- Relax and prepare to listen to the instructions
- If you have any physical problem that may keep you from doing your best, be sure to tell the test administrator. If you are sick or in poor health, you really cannot do your best on the exam. You can come back and take the test some other time.

VII. AT THE TEST

The day of the test is here and you have the test booklet in your hand. The temptation to get going is very strong. Caution! There is more to success than knowing the right answers. You must know how to identify your papers and understand variations in the type of short-answer question used in this particular examination. Follow these suggestions for maximum results from your efforts:

1) Cooperate with the monitor

The test administrator has a duty to create a situation in which you can be as much at ease as possible. He will give instructions, tell you when to begin, check to see that you are marking your answer sheet correctly, and so on. He is not there to guard you, although he will see that your competitors do not take unfair advantage. He wants to help you do your best.

2) Listen to all instructions

Don't jump the gun! Wait until you understand all directions. In most civil service tests you get more time than you need to answer the questions. So don't be in a hurry. Read each word of instructions until you clearly understand the meaning. Study the examples, listen to all announcements and follow directions. Ask questions if you do not understand what to do.

3) Identify your papers

Civil service exams are usually identified by number only. You will be assigned a number; you must not put your name on your test papers. Be sure to copy your number correctly. Since more than one exam may be given, copy your exact examination title.

4) Plan your time

Unless you are told that a test is a "speed" or "rate of work" test, speed itself is usually not important. Time enough to answer all the questions will be provided, but this does not mean that you have all day. An overall time limit has been set. Divide the total time (in minutes) by the number of questions to determine the approximate time you have for each question.

5) Do not linger over difficult questions

If you come across a difficult question, mark it with a paper clip (useful to have along) and come back to it when you have been through the booklet. One caution if you do this – be sure to skip a number on your answer sheet as well. Check often to be sure that you have not lost your place and that you are marking in the row numbered the same as the question you are answering.

6) Read the questions

Be sure you know what the question asks! Many capable people are unsuccessful because they failed to *read* the questions correctly.

7) Answer all questions

Unless you have been instructed that a penalty will be deducted for incorrect answers, it is better to guess than to omit a question.

8) Speed tests

It is often better NOT to guess on speed tests. It has been found that on timed tests people are tempted to spend the last few seconds before time is called in marking answers at random – without even reading them – in the hope of picking up a few extra points. To discourage this practice, the instructions may warn you that your score will be "corrected" for guessing. That is, a penalty will be applied. The incorrect answers will be deducted from the correct ones, or some other penalty formula will be used.

9) Review your answers

If you finish before time is called, go back to the questions you guessed or omitted to give them further thought. Review other answers if you have time.

10) Return your test materials

If you are ready to leave before others have finished or time is called, take ALL your materials to the monitor and leave quietly. Never take any test material with you. The monitor can discover whose papers are not complete, and taking a test booklet may be grounds for disqualification.

VIII. EXAMINATION TECHNIQUES

1) Read the general instructions carefully. These are usually printed on the first page of the exam booklet. As a rule, these instructions refer to the timing of the examination; the fact that you should not start work until the signal and must stop work at a signal, etc. If there are any *special* instructions, such as a choice of questions to be answered, make sure that you note this instruction carefully.

2) When you are ready to start work on the examination, that is as soon as the signal has been given, read the instructions to each question booklet, underline any key words or phrases, such as *least, best, outline, describe* and the like. In this way you will tend to answer as requested rather than discover on reviewing your paper that you *listed without describing*, that you selected the *worst* choice rather than the *best* choice, etc.

3) If the examination is of the objective or multiple-choice type – that is, each question will also give a series of possible answers: A, B, C or D, and you are called upon to select the best answer and write the letter next to that answer on your answer paper – it is advisable to start answering each question in turn. There may be anywhere from 50 to 100 such questions in the three or four hours allotted and you can see how much time would be taken if you read through all the questions before beginning to answer any. Furthermore, if you come across a question or group of questions which you know would be difficult to answer, it would undoubtedly affect your handling of all the other questions.

4) If the examination is of the essay type and contains but a few questions, it is a moot point as to whether you should read all the questions before starting to answer any one. Of course, if you are given a choice – say five out of seven and the like – then it is essential to read all the questions so you can eliminate the two that are most difficult. If, however, you are asked to answer all the questions, there may be danger in trying to answer the easiest one first because you may find that you will spend too much time on it. The best technique is to answer the first question, then proceed to the second, etc.

5) Time your answers. Before the exam begins, write down the time it started, then add the time allowed for the examination and write down the time it must be completed, then divide the time available somewhat as follows:

- If 3-1/2 hours are allowed, that would be 210 minutes. If you have 80 objective-type questions, that would be an average of 2-1/2 minutes per question. Allow yourself no more than 2 minutes per question, or a total of 160 minutes, which will permit about 50 minutes to review.
- If for the time allotment of 210 minutes there are 7 essay questions to answer, that would average about 30 minutes a question. Give yourself only 25 minutes per question so that you have about 35 minutes to review.

6) The most important instruction is to *read each question* and make sure you know what is wanted. The second most important instruction is to *time yourself properly* so that you answer every question. The third most important instruction is to *answer every question*. Guess if you have to but include something for each question. Remember that you will receive no credit for a blank and will probably receive some credit if you write something in answer to an essay question. If you guess a letter – say "B" for a multiple-choice question – you may have guessed right. If you leave a blank as an answer to a multiple-choice question, the examiners may respect your feelings but it will not add a point to your score. Some exams may penalize you for wrong answers, so in such cases *only*, you may not want to guess unless you have some basis for your answer.

7) Suggestions
   a. Objective-type questions
      1. Examine the question booklet for proper sequence of pages and questions
      2. Read all instructions carefully
      3. Skip any question which seems too difficult; return to it after all other questions have been answered
      4. Apportion your time properly; do not spend too much time on any single question or group of questions
      5. Note and underline key words – *all, most, fewest, least, best, worst, same, opposite,* etc.
      6. Pay particular attention to negatives
      7. Note unusual option, e.g., unduly long, short, complex, different or similar in content to the body of the question
      8. Observe the use of "hedging" words – *probably, may, most likely,* etc.
      9. Make sure that your answer is put next to the same number as the question
      10. Do not second-guess unless you have good reason to believe the second answer is definitely more correct
      11. Cross out original answer if you decide another answer is more accurate; do not erase until you are ready to hand your paper in
      12. Answer all questions; guess unless instructed otherwise
      13. Leave time for review

   b. Essay questions
      1. Read each question carefully
      2. Determine exactly what is wanted. Underline key words or phrases.
      3. Decide on outline or paragraph answer

4. Include many different points and elements unless asked to develop any one or two points or elements
5. Show impartiality by giving pros and cons unless directed to select one side only
6. Make and write down any assumptions you find necessary to answer the questions
7. Watch your English, grammar, punctuation and choice of words
8. Time your answers; don't crowd material

8) Answering the essay question

Most essay questions can be answered by framing the specific response around several key words or ideas. Here are a few such key words or ideas:

M's: manpower, materials, methods, money, management
P's: purpose, program, policy, plan, procedure, practice, problems, pitfalls, personnel, public relations

a. Six basic steps in handling problems:
1. Preliminary plan and background development
2. Collect information, data and facts
3. Analyze and interpret information, data and facts
4. Analyze and develop solutions as well as make recommendations
5. Prepare report and sell recommendations
6. Install recommendations and follow up effectiveness

b. Pitfalls to avoid
1. *Taking things for granted* – A statement of the situation does not necessarily imply that each of the elements is necessarily true; for example, a complaint may be invalid and biased so that all that can be taken for granted is that a complaint has been registered
2. *Considering only one side of a situation* – Wherever possible, indicate several alternatives and then point out the reasons you selected the best one
3. *Failing to indicate follow up* – Whenever your answer indicates action on your part, make certain that you will take proper follow-up action to see how successful your recommendations, procedures or actions turn out to be
4. *Taking too long in answering any single question* – Remember to time your answers properly

IX. AFTER THE TEST

Scoring procedures differ in detail among civil service jurisdictions although the general principles are the same. Whether the papers are hand-scored or graded by machine we have described, they are nearly always graded by number. That is, the person who marks the paper knows only the number – never the name – of the applicant. Not until all the papers have been graded will they be matched with names. If other tests, such as training and experience or oral interview ratings have been given, scores will be combined. Different parts of the examination usually have different weights. For example, the written test might count 60 percent of the final grade, and a rating of training and experience 40 percent. In many jurisdictions, veterans will have a certain number of points added to their grades.

After the final grade has been determined, the names are placed in grade order and an eligible list is established. There are various methods for resolving ties between those who get the same final grade – probably the most common is to place first the name of the person whose application was received first. Job offers are made from the eligible list in the order the names appear on it. You will be notified of your grade and your rank as soon as all these computations have been made. This will be done as rapidly as possible.

People who are found to meet the requirements in the announcement are called "eligibles." Their names are put on a list of eligible candidates. An eligible's chances of getting a job depend on how high he stands on this list and how fast agencies are filling jobs from the list.

When a job is to be filled from a list of eligibles, the agency asks for the names of people on the list of eligibles for that job. When the civil service commission receives this request, it sends to the agency the names of the three people highest on this list. Or, if the job to be filled has specialized requirements, the office sends the agency the names of the top three persons who meet these requirements from the general list.

The appointing officer makes a choice from among the three people whose names were sent to him. If the selected person accepts the appointment, the names of the others are put back on the list to be considered for future openings.

That is the rule in hiring from all kinds of eligible lists, whether they are for typist, carpenter, chemist, or something else. For every vacancy, the appointing officer has his choice of any one of the top three eligibles on the list. This explains why the person whose name is on top of the list sometimes does not get an appointment when some of the persons lower on the list do. If the appointing officer chooses the second or third eligible, the No. 1 eligible does not get a job at once, but stays on the list until he is appointed or the list is terminated.

X. HOW TO PASS THE INTERVIEW TEST

The examination for which you applied requires an oral interview test. You have already taken the written test and you are now being called for the interview test – the final part of the formal examination.

You may think that it is not possible to prepare for an interview test and that there are no procedures to follow during an interview. Our purpose is to point out some things you can do in advance that will help you and some good rules to follow and pitfalls to avoid while you are being interviewed.

What is an interview supposed to test?

The written examination is designed to test the technical knowledge and competence of the candidate; the oral is designed to evaluate intangible qualities, not readily measured otherwise, and to establish a list showing the relative fitness of each candidate – as measured against his competitors – for the position sought. Scoring is not on the basis of "right" and "wrong," but on a sliding scale of values ranging from "not passable" to "outstanding." As a matter of fact, it is possible to achieve a relatively low score without a single "incorrect" answer because of evident weakness in the qualities being measured.

Occasionally, an examination may consist entirely of an oral test – either an individual or a group oral. In such cases, information is sought concerning the technical knowledges and abilities of the candidate, since there has been no written examination for this purpose. More commonly, however, an oral test is used to supplement a written examination.

Who conducts interviews?

The composition of oral boards varies among different jurisdictions. In nearly all, a representative of the personnel department serves as chairman. One of the members of the board may be a representative of the department in which the candidate would work. In some cases, "outside experts" are used, and, frequently, a businessman or some other representative of the general public is asked to serve. Labor and management or other special groups may be represented. The aim is to secure the services of experts in the appropriate field.

However the board is composed, it is a good idea (and not at all improper or unethical) to ascertain in advance of the interview who the members are and what groups they represent. When you are introduced to them, you will have some idea of their backgrounds and interests, and at least you will not stutter and stammer over their names.

What should be done before the interview?

While knowledge about the board members is useful and takes some of the surprise element out of the interview, there is other preparation which is more substantive. It *is* possible to prepare for an oral interview – in several ways:

1) Keep a copy of your application and review it carefully before the interview

This may be the only document before the oral board, and the starting point of the interview. Know what education and experience you have listed there, and the sequence and dates of all of it. Sometimes the board will ask you to review the highlights of your experience for them; you should not have to hem and haw doing it.

2) Study the class specification and the examination announcement

Usually, the oral board has one or both of these to guide them. The qualities, characteristics or knowledges required by the position sought are stated in these documents. They offer valuable clues as to the nature of the oral interview. For example, if the job involves supervisory responsibilities, the announcement will usually indicate that knowledge of modern supervisory methods and the qualifications of the candidate as a supervisor will be tested. If so, you can expect such questions, frequently in the form of a hypothetical situation which you are expected to solve. NEVER go into an oral without knowledge of the duties and responsibilities of the job you seek.

3) Think through each qualification required

Try to visualize the kind of questions you would ask if you were a board member. How well could you answer them? Try especially to appraise your own knowledge and background in each area, *measured against the job sought*, and identify any areas in which you are weak. Be critical and realistic – do not flatter yourself.

4) Do some general reading in areas in which you feel you may be weak
For example, if the job involves supervision and your past experience has NOT, some general reading in supervisory methods and practices, particularly in the field of human relations, might be useful. Do NOT study agency procedures or detailed manuals. The oral board will be testing your understanding and capacity, not your memory.

5) Get a good night's sleep and watch your general health and mental attitude
You will want a clear head at the interview. Take care of a cold or any other minor ailment, and of course, no hangovers.

What should be done on the day of the interview?
Now comes the day of the interview itself. Give yourself plenty of time to get there. Plan to arrive somewhat ahead of the scheduled time, particularly if your appointment is in the fore part of the day. If a previous candidate fails to appear, the board might be ready for you a bit early. By early afternoon an oral board is almost invariably behind schedule if there are many candidates, and you may have to wait. Take along a book or magazine to read, or your application to review, but leave any extraneous material in the waiting room when you go in for your interview. In any event, relax and compose yourself.

The matter of dress is important. The board is forming impressions about you – from your experience, your manners, your attitude, and your appearance. Give your personal appearance careful attention. Dress your best, but not your flashiest. Choose conservative, appropriate clothing, and be sure it is immaculate. This is a business interview, and your appearance should indicate that you regard it as such. Besides, being well groomed and properly dressed will help boost your confidence.

Sooner or later, someone will call your name and escort you into the interview room. *This is it.* From here on you are on your own. It is too late for any more preparation. But remember, you asked for this opportunity to prove your fitness, and you are here because your request was granted.

What happens when you go in?
The usual sequence of events will be as follows: The clerk (who is often the board stenographer) will introduce you to the chairman of the oral board, who will introduce you to the other members of the board. Acknowledge the introductions before you sit down. Do not be surprised if you find a microphone facing you or a stenotypist sitting by. Oral interviews are usually recorded in the event of an appeal or other review.

Usually the chairman of the board will open the interview by reviewing the highlights of your education and work experience from your application – primarily for the benefit of the other members of the board, as well as to get the material into the record. Do not interrupt or comment unless there is an error or significant misinterpretation; if that is the case, do not hesitate. But do not quibble about insignificant matters. Also, he will usually ask you some question about your education, experience or your present job – partly to get you to start talking and to establish the interviewing "rapport." He may start the actual questioning, or turn it over to one of the other members. Frequently, each member undertakes the questioning on a particular area, one in which he is perhaps most competent, so you can expect each member to participate in the examination. Because time is limited, you may also expect some rather abrupt switches in the direction the questioning takes, so do not be upset by it. Normally, a board member will not pursue a single line of questioning unless he discovers a particular strength or weakness.

After each member has participated, the chairman will usually ask whether any member has any further questions, then will ask you if you have anything you wish to add. Unless you are expecting this question, it may floor you. Worse, it may start you off on an extended, extemporaneous speech. The board is not usually seeking more information. The question is principally to offer you a last opportunity to present further qualifications or to indicate that you have nothing to add. So, if you feel that a significant qualification or characteristic has been overlooked, it is proper to point it out in a sentence or so. Do not compliment the board on the thoroughness of their examination – they have been sketchy, and you know it. If you wish, merely say, "No thank you, I have nothing further to add." This is a point where you can "talk yourself out" of a good impression or fail to present an important bit of information. Remember, *you close the interview yourself.*

The chairman will then say, "That is all, Mr. _____, thank you." Do not be startled; the interview is over, and quicker than you think. Thank him, gather your belongings and take your leave. Save your sigh of relief for the other side of the door.

How to put your best foot forward

Throughout this entire process, you may feel that the board individually and collectively is trying to pierce your defenses, seek out your hidden weaknesses and embarrass and confuse you. Actually, this is not true. They are obliged to make an appraisal of your qualifications for the job you are seeking, and they want to see you in your best light. Remember, they must interview all candidates and a non-cooperative candidate may become a failure in spite of their best efforts to bring out his qualifications. Here are 15 suggestions that will help you:

1) Be natural – Keep your attitude confident, not cocky

If you are not confident that you can do the job, do not expect the board to be. Do not apologize for your weaknesses, try to bring out your strong points. The board is interested in a positive, not negative, presentation. Cockiness will antagonize any board member and make him wonder if you are covering up a weakness by a false show of strength.

2) Get comfortable, but don't lounge or sprawl

Sit erectly but not stiffly. A careless posture may lead the board to conclude that you are careless in other things, or at least that you are not impressed by the importance of the occasion. Either conclusion is natural, even if incorrect. Do not fuss with your clothing, a pencil or an ashtray. Your hands may occasionally be useful to emphasize a point; do not let them become a point of distraction.

3) Do not wisecrack or make small talk

This is a serious situation, and your attitude should show that you consider it as such. Further, the time of the board is limited – they do not want to waste it, and neither should you.

4) Do not exaggerate your experience or abilities

In the first place, from information in the application or other interviews and sources, the board may know more about you than you think. Secondly, you probably will not get away with it. An experienced board is rather adept at spotting such a situation, so do not take the chance.

5) If you know a board member, do not make a point of it, yet do not hide it

Certainly you are not fooling him, and probably not the other members of the board. Do not try to take advantage of your acquaintanceship – it will probably do you little good.

6) Do not dominate the interview

Let the board do that. They will give you the clues – do not assume that you have to do all the talking. Realize that the board has a number of questions to ask you, and do not try to take up all the interview time by showing off your extensive knowledge of the answer to the first one.

7) Be attentive

You only have 20 minutes or so, and you should keep your attention at its sharpest throughout. When a member is addressing a problem or question to you, give him your undivided attention. Address your reply principally to him, but do not exclude the other board members.

8) Do not interrupt

A board member may be stating a problem for you to analyze. He will ask you a question when the time comes. Let him state the problem, and wait for the question.

9) Make sure you understand the question

Do not try to answer until you are sure what the question is. If it is not clear, restate it in your own words or ask the board member to clarify it for you. However, do not haggle about minor elements.

10) Reply promptly but not hastily

A common entry on oral board rating sheets is "candidate responded readily," or "candidate hesitated in replies." Respond as promptly and quickly as you can, but do not jump to a hasty, ill-considered answer.

11) Do not be peremptory in your answers

A brief answer is proper – but do not fire your answer back. That is a losing game from your point of view. The board member can probably ask questions much faster than you can answer them.

12) Do not try to create the answer you think the board member wants

He is interested in what kind of mind you have and how it works – not in playing games. Furthermore, he can usually spot this practice and will actually grade you down on it.

13) Do not switch sides in your reply merely to agree with a board member

Frequently, a member will take a contrary position merely to draw you out and to see if you are willing and able to defend your point of view. Do not start a debate, yet do not surrender a good position. If a position is worth taking, it is worth defending.

14) Do not be afraid to admit an error in judgment if you are shown to be wrong
   The board knows that you are forced to reply without any opportunity for careful consideration. Your answer may be demonstrably wrong. If so, admit it and get on with the interview.

15) Do not dwell at length on your present job
   The opening question may relate to your present assignment. Answer the question but do not go into an extended discussion. You are being examined for a *new* job, not your present one. As a matter of fact, try to phrase ALL your answers in terms of the job for which you are being examined.

Basis of Rating
   Probably you will forget most of these "do's" and "don'ts" when you walk into the oral interview room. Even remembering them all will not ensure you a passing grade. Perhaps you did not have the qualifications in the first place. But remembering them will help you to put your best foot forward, without treading on the toes of the board members.
   Rumor and popular opinion to the contrary notwithstanding, an oral board wants you to make the best appearance possible. They know you are under pressure – but they also want to see how you respond to it as a guide to what your reaction would be under the pressures of the job you seek. They will be influenced by the degree of poise you display, the personal traits you show and the manner in which you respond.

ABOUT THIS BOOK

   This book contains tests divided into Examination Sections. Go through each test, answering every question in the margin. At the end of each test look at the answer key and check your answers. On the ones you got wrong, look at the right answer choice and learn. Do not fill in the answers first. Do not memorize the questions and answers, but understand the answer and principles involved. On your test, the questions will likely be different from the samples. Questions are changed and new ones added. If you understand these past questions you should have success with any changes that arise. Tests may consist of several types of questions. We have additional books on each subject should more study be advisable or necessary for you. Finally, the more you study, the better prepared you will be. This book is intended to be the last thing you study before you walk into the examination room. Prior study of relevant texts is also recommended. NLC publishes some of these in our Fundamental Series. Knowledge and good sense are important factors in passing your exam. Good luck also helps. So now study this Passbook, absorb the material contained within and take that knowledge into the examination. Then do your best to pass that exam.

EXAMINATION SECTION

EXAMINATION SECTION
TEST 1

DIRECTIONS: Each question or incomplete statement is followed by several suggested answers or completions. Select the one that BEST answers the question or completes the statement. *PRINT THE LETTER OF THE CORRECT ANSWER IN THE SPACE AT THE RIGHT.*

1. The purchase of goods *as is* includes a(n) 1.____

    A. warranty
    B. guarantee
    C. assurance of the condition of the goods
    D. assurance of the quantity available

2. A change order becomes legally binding after approval by the 2.____

    A. agency involved and the buyer
    B. buyer alone
    C. vendor alone
    D. chief purchasing officer and the vendor

3. Of the following courses of action, the MOST advisable one for a buyer to take in order to obtain an item costing under $100 in the shortest time possible would be to 3.____

    A. call in several vendors with whom he has dealt previously and discuss price and availability of the item
    B. invite all vendors who carry the item to submit written bids
    C. consult the classified telephone directory to find a local vendor and purchase the item directly
    D. try to locate the item in another agency's storehouse

4. A buyer SHOULD begin his analysis of bids by 4.____

    A. tabulating the bids received
    B. checking on the responsibility of all the bidders
    C. selecting the apparently high bids for consideration
    D. eliminating the bids from suppliers who have been consistently high bidders in the past

5. A buyer should make a recommendation for the award of a contract to the supplier who offers the 5.____

    A. lowest price
    B. suitable quality
    C. suitable quality and lowest price
    D. best value

6. Before recommending that a low bidder be awarded a contract for a certain commodity, a buyer SHOULD 6.____

A. ask other buyers what they consider a reasonable price for that commodity
B. check the low bidder's price against price indices to make sure that it is reasonable
C. make sure that he does not recommend accepting a bid at a higher price than that which was paid the last time the item was purchased
D. tell the bidder that he has a better chance of winning the contract if he will lower his price

7. When purchases are made by brand name, it USUALLY follows that the 7.____

A. buyer does not has to be concerned with the quality of the commodity
B. brand name commodity is superior in quality to other materials in the field
C. buyer depends upon the integrity and reliability of the company that produces the commodity
D. buyer is not required to advertise for bids on the commodity

8. Assume that a buyer asks for informal written quotations for a certain quantity of a commodity from four suppliers. He receives almost identical bids. He suspects collusion. In this situation, it would be MOST advisable for the buyer to 8.____

A. attempt to get four additional suppliers to bid
B. draw lots to determine the successful bidder
C. ask each supplier to rebid on the same specifications
D. reject all bids, revise specifications, and advertise for new bids

9. Of the following, the MOST important reason for a buyer to place contracts or purchase orders only with responsible bidders is that 9.____

A. the buyer may be blamed if a bidder defaults
B. irresponsible bidders usually charge high prices
C. if a bidder defaults, the agency involved may be without supplies during the time it takes to accept new bids
D. a responsible bidder always supplies goods of superior quality

10. Suppose that sealed bids are received from four suppliers. Supplier A bid $1 per unit; the next lowest bid was $1.12 per unit. The award is made to Supplier A. After receiving the contract, Supplier A tells the buyer that he made a mistake in his price and it should have been 10% higher.
In this situation, it would be BEST for the buyer to 10.____

A. rebid the entire requirement
B. agree to pay $1.10 per unit to Supplier A
C. disqualify Supplier A and award the contract to the supplier who bid $1.12 per unit
D. insist that Supplier A fill the order at $1 per unit or recommend that the order be cancelled and charge him the cost of obtaining the goods elsewhere

11. *Or equal* bidding requires that awards be 11.____

A. made only on the basis of samples submitted by the bidder
B. based upon comparative prices
C. made only where essential characteristics of the goods comply with specifications advertised
D. made only after bids from at least three regular suppliers have been considered and rejected

12. Suppose that a salesman sends a buyer tickets for six box seats at a World Series baseball game.
    In this situation, it would be MOST advisable for the buyer to

    A. divide the tickets among the purchasing department personnel
    B. donate the tickets to a charitable institution
    C. return the tickets to the salesman
    D. use the tickets to entertain visiting purchasing personnel

13. Which one of the following actions is ordinarily considered ACCEPTABLE purchasing practice?

    A. Asking for quotations from six suppliers and then deciding not to order any of the commodity
    B. Taking a cash discount of 2%, offered under 2/10 net 30, thirty days after receipt of the invoice and the material
    C. Requesting a quotation for 2,000 lbs. of paper and then ordering 125 lbs. at the 2,000 lb. price
    D. Asking a supplier for a sample of an item to fill an agency's need for only one of the items

14. Suppose that a purchase order for $50,000 of steel is placed, specifying delivery via barge. The price quoted includes cost of delivery and the terms are 2% 10 days. The invoice is dated April 1, and it arrives on April 3. A bill of lading for the shipment is dated April 4, and the steel arrives May 20.
    The 2% cash discount may be taken if the invoice is paid within 10 days after

    A. May 20   B. April 4   C. April 3   D. April 1

15. The term *caveat emptor* means:

    A. Let the seller beware
    B. The seller guarantees the quality
    C. Let the buyer beware
    D. Let the seller warrant the item

16. Which one of the following is NOT conducive to good communications between city purchasing personnel and suppliers?
    A

    A. friendly manner   B. firm but courteous manner
    C. personal approach   D. curt and brisk manner

17. You may, on occasion, interview vendors who wish to be placed on the bidder's list.
    When conducting such an interview, it would generally be considered MOST appropriate for you to

    A. imply that the vendor is likely to receive a number of contract awards if he submits a lot of bids
    B. stress that the vendor will have a lot of competition
    C. explain the bid process and answer the vendor's questions
    D. try to determine whether the vendor will actually submit any bids

18. Suppose that a buyer receives a request from a vendor for information which the buyer knows is confidential.
In this situation, it would usually be MOST desirable for the buyer to

18.____

   A. tell the vendor that the information he is asking for is confidential
   B. give the vendor the information in order to maintain friendly relations with him
   C. rebuke the vendor for asking for confidential information
   D. tell the vendor to call the supervising buyer in order to obtain the information

19. Suppose that a vendor who has bid for the first time is not awarded the contract. He calls you to complain, claiming that he offered exactly what the bid proposal specified.
In this situation, it would usually be MOST desirable for you to tell this vendor

19.____

   A. that all bids are carefully analyzed, and if he had deserved the award, he would have gotten it
   B. that if he is not satisfied with the decision he need not submit any bids in the future
   C. to submit other bids in the future, and he will surely be successful
   D. how bids are analyzed and why his bid was rejected

20. Suppose that you have been working as a buyer for a short time. You have a question regarding a purchase transaction you are handling, and, because your supervisor is not available at the time, you ask a fellow buyer how to proceed. The procedure he tells you to follow seems contrary to previous instructions you have received.
In this situation, the one of the following courses of action it would usually be BEST for you to follow would be to

20.____

   A. tell your fellow worker that he is giving you incorrect information
   B. thank your fellow worker for his assistance and wait for your supervisor to be available before proceeding
   C. ask your fellow worker if he will handle the purchase transaction for you
   D. follow the procedure your fellow worker told you and if it proves to be incorrect, explain to your supervisor that you were given wrong information by your fellow worker

KEY (CORRECT ANSWERS)

1.	D	11.	C
2.	D	12.	C
3.	C	13.	A
4.	A	14.	D
5.	C	15.	C
6.	B	16.	D
7.	C	17.	C
8.	D	18.	A
9.	C	19.	D
10.	D	20.	B

TEST 2

DIRECTIONS: Each question or incomplete statement is followed by several suggested answers or completions. Select the one that BEST answers the question or completes the statement. *PRINT THE LETTER OF THE CORRECT ANSWER IN THE SPACE AT THE RIGHT.*

1. Suppose that you purchase 100 units of an item at a list of $1 per unit less 40% and 10%, and less 2% if paid within 10 days.
   If payment is made within the ten-day limit, the amount of the payment would be

   A. $52.92   B. $54.00   C. $58.80   D. $60.00

   1._____

2. Another way of saying 1 3/4 gross is

   A. 144 individual units
   B. 7 dozen
   C. 21 dozen
   D. 250 individual units

   2._____

3. Assume that a buyer had to purchase 40,000 lbs. of salt. Which one of the following bids SHOULD he accept, assuming quality, service, and delivery terms are all the same?

   A. 1¢ per pound, 2%-30 days
   B. 99¢ per 100 lbs., 1%-30 days
   C. $19 per ton, 1%-30 days
   D. $18 per ton, net-30 days

   3._____

4. Which one of the following four bids represents the BEST value, assuming delivery costs amount to $100?

   A. $1000 f.o.b. buyer, less 2%-10 days
   B. $900 f.o.b. seller, less 2%-10 days
   C. $975 delivered, net cash 30 days
   D. $990 f.o.b. buyer, less 1%-10 days

   4._____

5. Suppose that four suppliers make the following offers to sell 2,000 units of a particular commodity.
   Which one is the MOST advantageous proposal?

   A. $10 list, less 40% and 5%
   B. $5 cost, plus 20% to cover overhead and profit
   C. $10 list, less 20% and 20%
   D. $5 cost, plus 10% overhead and 10% for profit

   5._____

Questions 6-7.

DIRECTIONS: Answer Questions 6 and 7 SOLELY on the basis of the information contained in the following chart, which plots the average price of a commodity during the calendar years indicated.

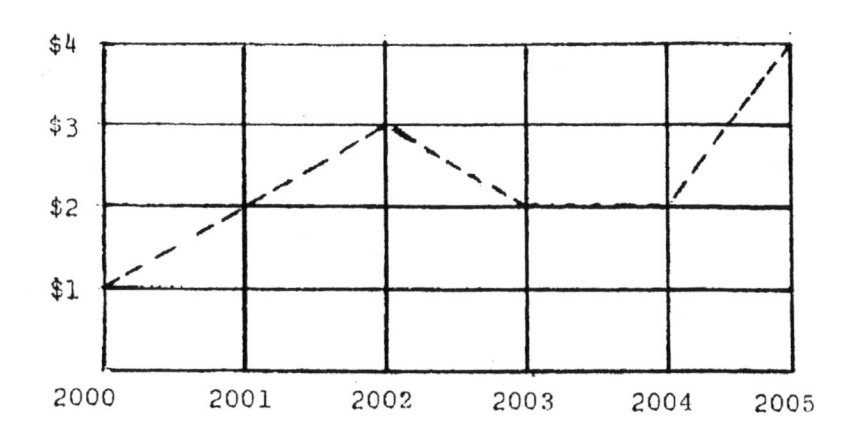

6. According to the above chart, the increase in the average price of the commodity from 2002 to 2005 was APPROXIMATELY

   A. 25%   B. 33 1/3%   C. 50%   D. 75%

7. According to the above chart, the increase in the average price of the commodity from 2000 to 2002 was APPROXIMATELY

   A. 20%   B. 30%   C. 200%   D. 300%

Questions 8-9.

DIRECTIONS: Answer Questions 8 and 9 SOLELY on the basis of the information contained in the chart below, which shows supply and demand of a commodity from January 1, 2001 to January 1, 2005.

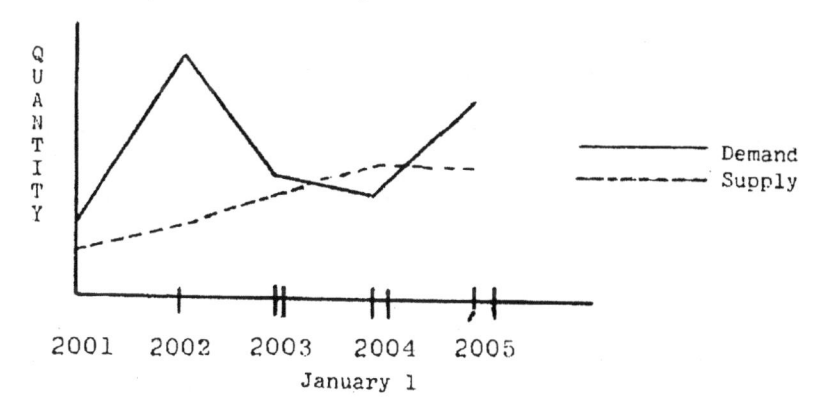

8. The above chart indicates that there was a seller's market during most of each of the following years EXCEPT

   A. 2001   B. 2002   C. 2003   D. 2004

9. According to the above chart, in the absence of price controls or other artificial or unusual circumstances, when would the price of the commodity have been the HIGHEST?
January 1,

   A. 2001   B. 2002   C. 2003   D. 2004

9.____

10. Assume that the 1967 cost of living factor was 100 and that a certain product was selling that year for $5 per unit. Assume further that at the present time, the cost of living factor is 150.
If the selling price of the product increased 10% more than the cost of living during this period, at the present time, the product would be selling for____ per unit.

   A. $8.25   B. $10.50   C. $16.50   D. $7.75

10.____

Questions 11-15.

DIRECTIONS: Questions 11 through 15 are to be answered on the basis of the instructions and paragraph which follow.

Instructions for answering Questions 11 through 15: The paragraph which follows is part of a report prepared by a buyer for submission to his superior.

The paragraph contains 5 underlined groups of words, each one bearing a number which identifies the question relating to it. Each of these groups of words MAY or MAY NOT represent correct written standard English suitable for use in a formal report. For each question, decide whether the group of words used in the paragraph which is always choice A, is correct written standard English and should be retained, or whether choice B, C, or D. Print the letter of the correct answer in the space at the right.

On October 23, 2005 the vendor delivered to microscopes to the using agency.

<u>When they inspected,</u> one microscope was found to have a defective part. The vendor
     11
was notified, and offered to replace the defective part; the using agency, however,

requested <u>that the microscope be replaced.</u> The vendor claimed that complete
            12
replacement was unnecessary and refused to comply with the agency's demand,

<u>having the result that the agency declared</u> that it will pay only for the acceptable
          13
microscope. At that point <u>I got involved by the agency's contacting me.</u> The agency
           14
requested that I speak to the vendor since I handled the original purchase and

<u>have dealed with this vendor before.</u>
     15

11. A. When they inspected,
    B. Upon inspection,
    C. The inspection report said that
    D. Having inspected,

12. A. that the microscope be replaced.
    B. a whole new microscope in replacement.
    C. to have a replacement for the microscope.
    D. that they get the microscope replaced.

13. A. , having the result that the agency declared
    B. ; the agency consequently declared
    C. , which refusal caused the agency to consequently declare
    D. , with the result of the agency's declaring

14. A. I got involved by the agency's contacting me.
    B. I became involved, being contacted by the agency.
    C. the agency contacting me, I got involved,
    D. the agency contacted me and I became involved.

15. A. have dealed with this vendor before.
    B. done business before with this vendor.
    C. know this vendor by prior dealings.
    D. have dealt with this vendor before.

Questions 16-18.

DIRECTIONS: Answer Questions 16 through 18 on the basis of the following letter, which was prepared by a buyer in response to a letter of inquiry from a prospective bidder.

Mr. Fred Stewart
XYZ Manufacturing Company
200 West Street
Chicago, Illinois 21783

Dear Mr. Stewart:

To answer your question—yes, sometimes the City buys things from out-of-town people. If you're really interested in bidding, the Office of Vendor Relations can send you some forms to fill out. Then you can get on the bidders list and you won't miss any chances to bid because we'll notify you automatically. You could just submit a bid, but before you could be awarded a contract you would have to fill out the forms anyway.

Hope this information answers your question.

Very truly yours,
John Jones

16. Which one of the following criticisms of the style in which the above letter is written is MOST appropriate?
    The

    A. A. language is ambiguous
    B. letter Hacks concreteness
    C. language is too colloquial
    D. letter is too brief

17. The impression that the recipient is MOST likely to get from the above letter is

    A. *favorable,* because the tone of the letter is friendly
    B. *unfavorable,* because of the unprofessional tone of the letter
    C. *favorable,* because the letter is encouraging
    D. *unfavorable,* because the letter is not sufficiently courteous

18. Of the following changes suggested to the buyer, which one would have MOST improved the above letter?

    A. Refer specifically to the recipient's original letter of inquiry
    B. Give all the infornmtion necessary for the recipient to take appropriate action
    C. Offer to send the recipient some informative literature
    D. Directly encourage the recipient to do business with the City

Questions 19-20.

DIRECTIONS: Base your answers to Questions 19 and 20 on the following passage.

   The City Charter requires that all purchases be made according to definite standards, or specifications. A specification may be defined as a statement of particulars descriptive of materials, or performance, or both; or, as a description of the technical details of a required commodity or service; or as a statement of what the buyer wants the seller to furnish. The specification should concisely define the quality of the commodity that is required to meet the needs of the using agency but still provide as wide competition in sources of supply as possible. To be of maximum value, the specification should describe the commodity clearly and in sufficient detail to ensure obtaining the exact commodity required.

19. Suppose that a buyer prepared the following specification for an item: cotton, absorbent, rolled.
    Based on the information given in the above passage, this specification would NOT be of value MAINLY because the

    A. quality of cotton required is not described
    B. description is not concise
    C. mode of packaging is not stated
    D. using agency is not referred to

20. Based on the information given in the above passage, the MOST important indication 20._____
that a specification has been well prepared is that the
   A. buyer gets few bids on the commodity
   B. commodity obtained meets the needs of the using agency
   C. commodity is procured at the lowest possible cost
   D. commodity is described in great detail

KEY (CORRECT ANSWERS)

1. A	11. B
2. C	12. A
3. D	13. B
4. C	14. D
5. A	15. D
6. B	16. C
7. C	17. B
8. C	18. B
9. B	19. A
10. A	20. B

EXAMINATION SECTION
TEST 1

DIRECTIONS: Each question or incomplete statement is followed by several suggested answers or completions. Select the one that BEST answers the question or completes the statement. *PRINT THE LETTER OF THE CORRECT ANSWER IN THE SPACE AT THE RIGHT.*

1. Of the following, the BEST advantage of centralized purchasing is that it is likely to result in
   A. lower unit costs of commodities
   B. a reduction in the number of personnel devoting time to purchasing
   C. more suppliers selling their commodities to the city
   D. less standardization of items used by the various city agencies

   1.____

2. All of the following are characteristics of a representative specification EXCEPT that the
   A. required quality is described clearly
   B. industry standards are utilized wherever possible
   C. criteria for testing upon delivery of goods are clearly described
   D. tolerances are drawn closer than those in industry standards to assure compliance with the specification

   2.____

3. Of the following, it is MOST important for agencies to anticipate their purchase requirements adequately so that the buyer may
   A. have time to search the market for the best value
   B. secure prices for larger quantities of the item needed
   C. have time to search the market for substitutes
   D. have time to search the market for seconds

   3.____

4. The one of the following which is a function of a purchasing procedure manual is to explain to
   A. potential vendors how to sell merchandise to the city
   B. agencies how to negotiate with vendors for their purchasing needs for materials, supplies, and equipment
   C. potential vendors which agencies will use certain commodities
   D. agencies how to request an item to be purchased and how the purchase will be accomplished

   4.____

5. The one of the following items which need NOT be included on a requisition submitted by an agency is the
   A. quality of the item needed
   B. description of the item needed
   C. name of the agency preparing the requisition
   D. name of the vendor from whom the item is to be purchased

   5.____

6. Which one of the following items is NOT a factor to be taken into consideration by a buyer when considering the suitability of a potential source of supply?
   A. Accessibility of the supplier
   B. Financial position of the supplier

   6.____

13

C. Cash discount items offered by the supplier
D. Reliability of the supplier

7. Which one of the following is the LEAST important reason for a buyer to initiate a purchase?
A(n)

   A. advertisement offers a bargain for a product used occasionally
   B. need for a commodity develops an agency
   C. minimum inventory is reached in a stock item in the storeroom
   D. construction project requires equipment for the completion of a building

8. If an agency requests the purchase of materials for a current renovation project, the LEAST important thing for a buyer to consider in handling this purchase transaction is

   A. quantity requirements
   B. when the materials will be delivered
   C. the kinds of materials required
   D. what type of renovation is being done

9. Acceptance of a sample from a potential supplier carries with it an obligation for the buyer to

   A. return it unused
   B. have the item inspected or tested and then have the supplier advised of the results
   C. retain it in the purchasing department
   D. purchase a quantity of the product

10. The one of the following factors which is NOT pertinent to consider in determining whether a bidder is responsible is the bidder's

    A. financial resources
    B. technical resources
    C. reputation among other buyers
    D. reputation among other suppliers

11. When may a sealed bid be changed by a potential supplier?

    A. Never
    B. Any time before the closing date
    C. After the closing date but before the bids are opened
    D. After the bids are opened but before an award is made

12. When a buyer asks for a quotation on an item that is specified in detail, he may accept a substitute ONLY if

    A. the item as specified is not manufactured in this country
    B. the item as specified is out of stock in the successful bidder's warehouse
    C. there is substantial compliance with the item as specified
    D. there was only one vendor who could supply the item as specified

13. The one of the following which should NOT be considered by a buyer when determining the low bid is the

    A. discount from list price B. f.o.b. terms
    C. advertised retail price   D. cash discount

14. In purchasing, the specification for a technical commodity which is to be purchased should be developed by the

    A. buyer alone
    B. buyer and the agency involved
    C. salesman for a potential supplier
    D. research department of a potential supplier

15. During a period of rising prices, which one of the following options would be MOST advisable for a buyer to select?

    A. *Price at the time of delivery* contracts
    B. *Hand to mouth* purchases
    C. Long term *fixed price* contracts
    D. *Spot* contracts

16. A standardization program is BEST established and has the MOST opportunity of succeeding if it is developed

    A. by representatives from successful suppliers in past years
    B. by the senior purchasing officers
    C. and approved by a committee of representatives from city agencies and the purchasing department
    D. by a citizens' committee

17. A purchase order that has been acknowledged and accepted by the vendor may be cancelled by the city if the

    A. city agency involved has no available funds in its budget
    B. buyer finds a cheaper substitute
    C. vendor agrees to accept a cancellation
    D. vendor submits an invoice before shipping the order

18. Assume that you have received four identical bids for a large quantity of a brand name item and it has been agreed that there is no good substitute for it.
    In this situation, you SHOULD recommend that the award be made to the supplier

    A. who sold the item to the city the last time it was purchased
    B. who originally brought the item to your attention
    C. who regularly advertises the product on television
    D. whose warehouse and office are located within the city limits

4 (#1)

19. Suppose that a buyer establishes the mode and routing of transportation of a purchased commodity.
The one of the following which is NOT a valid reason for doing so is to insure that the shipment arrives

19.____

   A. in top condition
   B. in returnable containers
   C. at the most economical cost
   D. on schedule

20. Suppose that a buyer has been asked to outfit a small room in an agency's building as a library. He asks Supplier X, who manufactures library equipment and has an architect on his staff, to develop a plan and suggest equipment for the room. Supplier X submits blueprints, equipment lists, and an installed price of $50,000. The agency is delighted with the proposed plan and approves it. It would then be MOST appropriate for the buyer to

20.____

   A. award the order to Supplier X
   B. pay Supplier X for the plans only and then ask Suppliers X, Y, and Z to bid on these plans
   C. ask Suppliers Y and Z to develop plans, then award the order to the low bidder of the three
   D. use Supplier X's plans and lists, ask Suppliers Y and Z to submit prices, and then award to the low bidder

KEY (CORRECT ANSWERS)

1.	A	11.	B
2.	D	12.	C
3.	A	13.	C
4.	D	14.	B
5.	D	15.	C
6.	C	16.	C
7.	A	17.	C
8.	D	18.	D
9.	B	19.	B
10.	D	20.	B

TEST 2

DIRECTIONS: Each question or incomplete statement is followed by several suggested answers or completions. Select the one that BEST answers the question or completes the statement. *PRINT THE LETTER OF THE CORRECT ANSWER IN THE SPACE AT THE RIGHT.*

1. Purchasing the proper quantity is a responsibility of a buyer. Buying small quantities at a time is likely to result in a reduction in the number of

    A. purchasing personnel
    B. purchase orders issued
    C. quantity price discounts received
    D. invoices to be paid

    1.____

2. Of the following factors, the one that should NOT be considered by a buyer when determining the quantity of an item to be ordered is the

    A. quantity price differentials
    B. cash discount terms offered
    C. rate of past use
    D. shelf life or possible deterioration if kept in inventory too long

    2.____

3. A buyer may make a purchase WITHOUT negotiation when

    A. the commodity has been purchased previously without negotiation
    B. the commodity costs relatively little in dollars and cents
    C. a requirement contract has been established for the commodity
    D. a brand name is required

    3.____

4. The one of the following which is the proper quality guide for a commodity to be purchased that will give the BEST value for the money expended is the

    A. quality suitable for the intended use
    B. best quality of the item
    C. cheapest quality available
    D. best quality manufactured locally

    4.____

5. Which one of the following would NOT constitute proper use of a buyer's association with a salesman?

    A. Develop interest in all the salesman's products among city agencies
    B. Accelerate delivery of the salesman's firm's product to meet a deadline
    C. Acquaint the buyer with the method by which the salesman's firm manufactures its product
    D. Acquaint the buyer with other products produced by the salesman's firm

    5.____

6. A supplier's catalog is GENERALLY regarded by a buyer or purchasing agent as a publication that

    A. lists the prices at which the products shown must be sold
    B. invites business with the firm for the products illustrated
    C. assures that the composition of the products will be maintained as described
    D. assures that the products illustrated are carried in stock

    6.____

7. One of the duties of a buyer is to maintain up-to-date mailing lists of prospective bidders. The BEST reason for maintaining such lists is that they

   A. make it unnecessary for the buyer to formally advertise for bids
   B. provide a convenient and accurate record of sources of supply
   C. enable a buyer to identify and eliminate vendors who have been consistently high bidders in the past
   D. provide a group of vendors who are sure to submit bids

8. Suppose that a city agency needs 20 one-gallon cans of cleaner.
   Which of the following MOST adequately describes the quantity needed? _____ cleaner

   A. 20 gallons   B. 80 quarts
   C. 4 five-gallon cans   D. 20 x 1 gallon cans of

9. *Expediting delivery* means

   A. assisting in unloading a shipment
   B. making certain that the supplier knows where to send the material
   C. offering containers in which the goods may be shipped
   D. taking action to assure delivery of goods purchased in accordance with a time schedule

10. Once a purchase order has been sent to the vendor, a buyer is NOT relieved of further responsibility until he has been notified that the

    A. agency wanted a different color of the item
    B. item was accepted
    C. time delivered did not meet specifications
    D. item was damaged on arrival

11. Which one of the following is the MOST important reason for stocking a commodity in a central storehouse?

    A. A local supplier can deliver about as quickly as the central storehouse.
    B. City agencies have not standardized the commodity.
    C. The commodity is used by the city agencies all during the year.
    D. Some city agencies lack space for storing the commodity.

12. Which one of the following describes a *seller's market*?

    A. Demand exceeds supply
    B. Supply exceeds demand
    C. Goods are easy to purchase
    D. The buyer demands and gets his price for the goods

13. The one of the following bonds which is NOT generally used in city purchasing is a _____ bond.

    A. surety   B. performance
    C. bid   D. payment

14. A buyer is MOST likely to obtain commodities of the proper quality at the right price if he   14._____

    A. consistently awards purchase orders to the lowest bidder
    B. carefully prepares specifications for required commodities
    C. accepts bids only from large suppliers
    D. purchases brand name commodities whenever possible

15. The term *f.o.b.* is a   15._____

    A. shipping term   B. trade discount term
    C. cash payment demand   D. quality term

16. Traffic, a purchasing responsibility, is defined as the   16._____

    A. method of delivery and routing of commodities ordered
    B. packaging of commodities ordered
    C. time of delivery of commodities ordered
    D. quantity of items to be delivered

17. A back order is a(n)   17._____

    A. order that is more than 90 days behind the scheduled delivery
    B. portion of an order the vendor cannot deliver at the scheduled time and has reentered for future delivery
    C. order that is repeated in identically the same terms as a previous order
    D. portion of an order that has been recalled and cancelled

18. The term *f.o.b. destination* signifies that it is the   18._____

    A. buyer's obligation and expense to get the goods from the seller's factory
    B. seller's obligation and expense to deliver the goods to the buyer
    C. seller's obligation to deliver the goods to the buyer at the buyer's expense
    D. buyer's duty to insure the merchandise against loss

19. When an *escalator clause* is used, it would ordinarily be found in a _____ contract.   19._____

    A. *fixed price*
    B. *spot*
    C. *price at the time of delivery*
    D. *cost plus*

20. In purchasing, lead time is GENERALLY considered to be the period of time from the date of   20._____

    A. order to date of delivery
    B. requisition to date of delivery
    C. quotation request to date of delivery
    D. requisition to date of order

KEY (CORRECT ANSWERS)

1. C
2. B
3. B
4. A
5. A

6. B
7. B
8. D
9. D
10. B

11. C
12. A
13. A
14. B
15. A

16. A
17. B
18. B
19. C
20. B

EXAMINATION SECTION
TEST 1

DIRECTIONS: Each question or incomplete statement is followed by several suggested answers or completions. Select the one that BEST answers the question or completes the statement. *PRINT THE LETTER OF THE CORRECT ANSWER IN THE SPACE AT THE RIGHT.*

Questions 1-8.

DIRECTIONS: Questions 1 through 8 are to be answered SOLELY on the basis of the following graph.

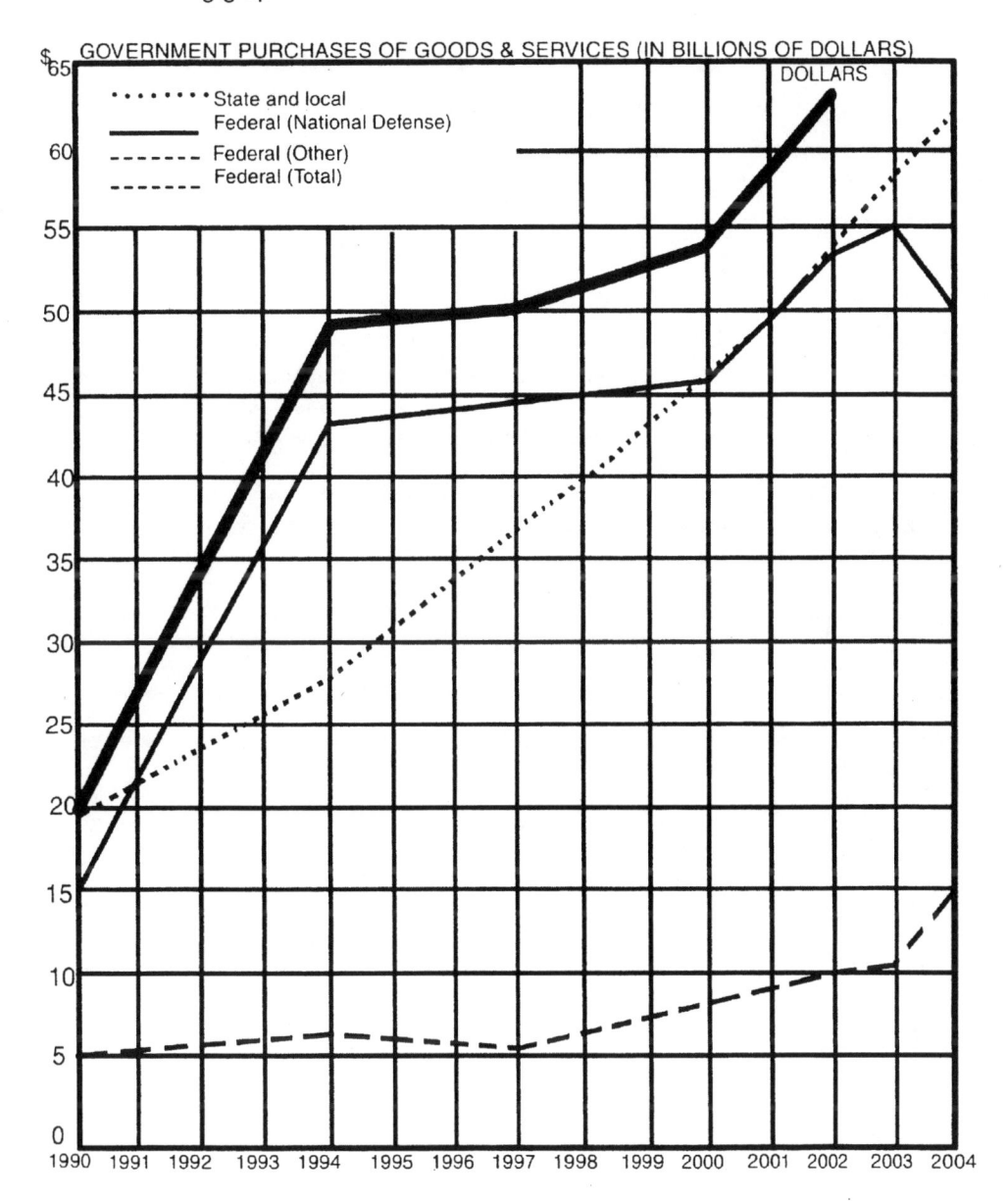

GOVERNMENT PURCHASES OF GOODS & SERVICES (IN BILLIONS OF DOLLARS)

- ······· State and local
- ——— Federal (National Defense)
- − − − − Federal (Other)
- - - - - - Federal (Total)

2 (#1)

1. Purchases by the Federal government for non-defense purposes, and purchases by State and local governments comprised the SMALLEST proportion of the total government purchases of goods and services for all purposes in which of the following years?

   A. 1990 B. 1994 C. 1997 D. 2000

2. Which one of the following MOST closely approximates the percentage increase in State and local purchases of goods and services in 2004 as compared with 1990?

   A. 110% B. 150% C. 220% D. 350%

3. Total government purchases of goods and services in 2004 was MOST NEARLY _____ billion dollars.

   A. 80 B. 110 C. 128 D. 144

4. In 2000, purchases made by State and local governments

   A. exceeded Federal government total purchases
   B. exceeded purchases made by them in 1994 by more than 50%
   C. increases less than 10% over 1997
   D. were less than 50% of purchases made by them in 2003

5. Purchases of goods and services for national defense in 1994 by the Federal government was MOST NEARLY

   A. 15% less than the total spent by Federal, State, and local governments for all purposes in 1990
   B. 50% of the total spent by Federal, State, and local governments for all purposes in 1997
   C. four times the amount spent in 1990 for national defense
   D. ten times the amount spent in 1994 by the Federal government for purposes other than national defense

6. In which one of the following years did State and local purchases of goods and services comprise the GREATEST proportion of the total spent by all government jurisdictions?

   A. 1990 B. 1994 C. 1997 D. 2002

7. The dollar increase in purchases of goods and services was LEAST for which one of the following?

   A. State and local governments between 1990 and 1994
   B. State and local governments between 1997 and 2000
   C. Total Federal government between 2000 and 2002
   D. Federal government other than national defense between 2000 and 2003

8. The rate of increase in Federal purchases of goods and services for national defense was GREATEST between which one of the following periods?
   From _____ to _____.

   A. 1994; 1997 B. 1997; 2000
   C. 2000; 2002 D. 2002; 2004

9. A uniform purchasing procedure is desirable in any well managed organization. Of the following, which statement as applied to a uniform purchasing procedure is LEAST valid?
A uniform purchasing procedure

   A. enables suitable documentation of transactions to meet the requirements of any auditing agency
   B. fosters good public relations in the community by giving many vendors an opportunity to bid on items
   C. generally permits low cost paper processing
   D. provides for spot-checking industrial operations so that quality control standards may be changed

10. A system of progress charting in the procurement of heavy major capital budget equipment would normally be LEAST useful in relation to procuring delivery on target date of which of the following?

   A. Fire Pumpers
   B. Garbage Collection Trucks
   C. Mimeograph Machines
   D. Police Cars

11. Standardization has the advantage of lowering the number of purchase orders and the quantity and variety of items to be stored.
The achievement of standardization is MOST generally the objective of

   A. design analysis
   B. lead time
   C. perpetual inventory
   D. reclamation procedures

12. Of the following, the LEAST desirable system for identifying standard commodities is the _____ system.

   A. alphabetic
   B. alphanumeric
   C. Dewey decimal
   D. non-sequential

13. Which one of the following influences LEAST the price level of commodities?

   A. Current market prices
   B. Seasonal trends
   C. Published quotations
   D. Storage restrictions

14. A manufacturer would be BEST advised to bypass the wholesaler or mill supply house when

   A. his product requires specialized selling and service
   B. his product has low value per unit
   C. his product has a demand situation similar to water
   D. he needs widespread distribution to a large number of outlets

15. The term *cost* usually includes all of the following EXCEPT

   A. any taxes applicable to the job payroll and any payment on bonds specified in the contract
   B. all overhead costs as defined and agreed to
   C. provision to add costs where the final profit margin falls outside limits considered to be reasonable
   D. cost of all material and labor services directly applicable to the job

16. Convenience goods are generally NOT characterized by which one of the following phrases?

    A. Bought frequently
    B. Minimum effort devoted to purchase
    C. Non-durable
    D. Purchase often postponed until more convenient time

17. Generally, what is the time limit for filing a claim with a carrier for concealed damage?

    A. 15 days   B. 30 days   C. 3 months   D. 1 year

18. Generally, what is the time limit for filing a loss or damage claim with a carrier?

    A. 15 days   B. 3 months   C. 9 months   D. 1 year

19. Of the following, the one which is NOT a reason for NOT making downpayments or progress payments is:

    A. If the item does not perform as required and promised, there may be difficulty in recovering monies paid
    B. Money is tied up before you have use of the item
    C. There is risk of losing the item and part of the payments made if the supplier goes bankrupt
    D. Specially designed machinery and equipment usually cannot be purchased under a contract requiring this method of payment

20. Generally, the impact upon the purchasing function of the use of an automated stock control system is to

    A. eliminate human judgment in determining reorder points
    B. reduce the amount of clerical work required
    C. reduce the need for maintaining safety stock levels
    D. require the drafting of more rigid specifications

21. A buyer who leaves equipment with a skilled worker for repair should be aware that the latter has a right to retain possession of the property until he is paid for the labor or materials he has bestowed on it.
    This right is called a(n)

    A. assignment   B. lien
    C. warrant of attachment   D. bailment

22. Prior to the issuance of orders to new (unlisted) vendors, of the following, it is MOST important to investigate the new vendors'

    A. competence to fulfill their obligations
    B. degree of in-plant mechanization
    C. choice of transportation vehicles
    D. discrimination against potential employees on an age basis

23. Analysis of bids for equipment buying does NOT include analysis of

    A. cost requirements   B. leasing methods
    C. performance efficiency D. specifications

5 (#1)

24. The one of the following which should normally be the MAJOR factor determining the signatory approvals required on a purchase requisition is the

   A. mode of transportation to be required to deliver the requisitioned items
   B. number of copies of the requisition required
   C. number of different commodity classes included on the requisition
   D. total dollar value of the items on the requisition

25. A statute that requires low dollar limitation on informal bids for open-market purchases is considered by purchasing officials to be generally

   A. *desirable*; it will increase the efficiency of the purchasing office
   B. *desirable;* it will reduce the incurrence of additional costs
   C. *undesirable*; it will cause unnecessary delays
   D. *undesirable;* it will result in a tendency to bypass local sources of supply

26. In preparing an annual requirement contract, the estimated quantity to be purchased should GENERALLY be

   A. inflated, in order to receive the lowest price possible
   B. comparable to the quantity purchased the previous year, unless it is expected that a greater quantity will be required for the ensuing year
   C. reduced, in order to allow for additional small orders in case of a drop in prices
   D. related to the quality specifications of the item

27. The MAJOR purpose of a price escalator clause in a contract is to

   A. define the rights of the seller and buyer if the seller cannot deliver merchandise of the quality, quantity, and at the price specified
   B. enable the buyer and seller to allocate elements of cost risk equitably between them
   C. enable the buyer to cancel the contract if costs of production exceed prices agreed upon
   D. ward off changes in price anticipated as a result of pending legislation or governmental regulation

28. Sales terms to Gideonburg, Ohio plant state that price is F.O.B. Dayton, Ohio, freight equalized with Akron, Ohio. At the buyer's request, freight is prepaid to New York City. In absence of any other provision in the agreement, titles will pass to the buyer at

   A. Akron   B. Dayton
   C. Gideonburg   D. New York City

29. A seller makes a false statement to a buyer of a material fact regarding certain merchandise which he is offering for sale. The statement is made with intent to deceive the buyer and induces him to enter into a contract which, had he not been misled, he would not have entered into. According to the above statement, which of the following statements is MOST valid?
The

   A. seller is guilty of misrepresentation which justifies rescission of the contract
   B. buyer may not have the contract rescinded, though
   C. he is entitled to receive compensation for any losses he has sustained

D. seller may enforce the contract if he can prove that his merchandise is as good as or better than the merchandise contracted for
E. buyer is guilty of misplaced confidence; he takes the risk of quality unless he protects himself by a warranty beforehand

30. Assume that you require 4 tons of fertilizer. The fertilizer is packed in 100 pound bags. Which of the following represents the LOWEST bid for the fertilizer?

   A. 6¢ per pound
   B. $5.50 per bag
   C. $7.00 for each of the first 30 bags; $5.00 for each bag thereafter
   D. $500.00 less discount

31. Assume pencils are packed 5 gross to the case. A buyer requires 3800 pencils each for three departments and 2700 pencils for another department. Assume that the vendor will ship unbroken cases only directly to each department.
How many cases should he buy?

   A. 21   B. 22   C. 48   D. 49

32. Printing from raised surface is done by which printing process?

   A. Debossing   B. Letterpress
   C. Offset lithography   D. Rotogravure

33. Of the following, the topic which is LEAST appropriate in a governmental purchasing manual is

   A. Buying for Employees   B. Ethics
   C. Training   D. Vendor Contacts

34. Which one of the following is LEAST appropriate as a program objective for a central purchasing agency?

   A. Decreasing the degree of mechanization of storehouse operations
   B. Developing a more meaningful training program for the buying staff
   C. Updating and delineating purchasing procedure for use by the agency's own staff and by using agency personnel concerned with procurement
   D. Relieving buyers of clerical duties so that they may concentrate more on the elevation of the quality and scope of purchasing activities

35. The use of an automated inventory control system GENERALLY results in

   A. an increase in the number of items kept in inventory
   B. greater utilization of available warehouse storage space
   C. the availability of more accurate perpetual inventory data
   D. the elimination of the need for physical inventories

36. For a buyer in charge of a section to ask occasionally the opinion of a subordinate concerning a buying problem is

   A. *desirable;* but it would be even better if the subordinate were consulted routinely on every buying problem
   B. *desirable;* subordinates may make good suggestions and will be pleased by being consulted

C. *undesirable;* subordinates may be resentful if their advice is not followed
D. *undesirable;* the buyer should not attempt to shift his responsibilities to subordinates

37. Generally, it is considered desirable practice to maintain stock at a three months level of supply.
Under what circumstances would it be MOST desirable to reduce stock levels to a one month period?

A. Discounts when buying larger quantities
B. Few obsolete items
C. Rapid deterioration of items
D. Rising prices

37.____

38. You find that delivery of a certain item cannot possibly be made to a using agency by the date the using agency requested.
Of the following, the MOST advisable course of action for you to take FIRST is to

A. cancel the order and inform the using agency
B. discuss the problem with the using agency
C. notify the using agency to obtain the item through direct purchase
D. schedule the delivery for the earliest possible date

38.____

39. Of the following classes of supplies, the one which you would expect to have the HIGHEST safety stock level is

A. foods
B. office machines
C. pharmaceuticals and drugs
D. spare parts

39.____

40. When a buyer delegates some of his work to a subordinate, the

A. buyer retains final responsibility for the work
B. buyer should not check on the work until it has been completed
C. subordinate assumes full responsibility for the successful completion of the work
D. subordinate is likely to lose interest and get less satisfaction from the work

40.____

KEY (CORRECT ANSWERS)

1.	B	11.	A	21.	B	31.	B
2.	C	12.	D	22.	A	32.	B
3.	C	13.	D	23.	B	33.	A
4.	B	14.	A	24.	D	34.	A
5.	B	15.	C	25.	C	35.	C
6.	A	16.	D	26.	B	36.	B
7.	D	17.	A	27.	B	37.	C
8.	C	18.	C	28.	B	38.	B
9.	D	19.	D	29.	A	39.	D
10.	C	20.	B	30.	B	40.	A

EXAMINATION SECTION
TEST 1

DIRECTIONS: Each question or incomplete statement is followed by several suggested answers or completions. Select the one that BEST answers the question or completes the statement. *PRINT THE LETTER OF THE CORRECT ANSWER IN THE SPACE AT THE RIGHT.*

1. A consignment sale is one in which the store and the vendor agree that the merchandise may be   1._____

    A. sold in installments
    B. sold at a cut price
    C. sold for cash only
    D. returned if unsold within a specified time

2. The cost at port of entry of goods purchased outside the country is its   2._____

    A. advalorem duty   B. specific duty
    C. landed cost   D. import tax

3. The difference between the net sales and the gross cost of merchandise sold is the   3._____

    A. maintained mark-up   B. initial mark-up
    C. legitimate mark-up   D. planned mark-up

4. The difference between the planned purchases of a department and the commitments already made for a specific control period is referred to as   4._____

    A. outstanding orders   B. planned purchases
    C. "open to buy"   D. purchase order list

5. An assortment of goods of different qualities and values, all offered for sale at a single reduced price, is a   5._____

    A. broken assortment   B. job lot
    C. special purchase   D. consignment lot

6. The price at which a product handled by competitors is generally sold is the   6._____

    A. market price   B. market-plus price
    C. market-minus price   D. retail price

7. If goods are bought on the installment plan, title passes from seller to buyer when the   7._____

    A. down payment is made   B. last installment is paid
    C. goods are half paid   D. goods are delivered

8. If goods are bought with the privilege of return, title passes from seller to buyer when the   8._____

    A. buyer makes up his mind   B. goods are paid for
    C. goods are delivered   D. sale is made

29

9. In a charge sale, title to the merchandise passes from seller to buyer when the   9.____

   A. goods are paid for   B. goods are delivered
   C. contract is made   D. goods are wrapped

10. In a cash sale, title to the merchandise passes from seller to buyer when the   10.____

    A. customer says "I'll take it"
    B. goods are wrapped
    C. goods are paid for
    D. goods are delivered

11. An oral contract for the purchase of a picture at $75 is enforceable if   11.____

    A. both parties agree
    B. part payment is made
    C. the picture was set aside
    D. the store got another one from the wholesaler

12. A contract for the sale of goods must be in writing when the amount is greater than   12.____
    _____ to be enforceable.

    A. $250   B. $350   C. $500   D. $400

13. A salesman's authority is defined by the law of   13.____

    A. contracts   B. agency
    C. sales   D. negotiables

14. The discount MOST usually allowed to stores by the ready-to-wear trade is   14.____

    A. 2/10 net 30   B. 8/10 E.O.M.
    C. 3/30   D. 2/10 60 X

15. The time allowed for payment of an invoice without deduction of discount is the   15.____

    A. discount period   B. net period
    C. net terms   D. payment period

16. Goods going from a factory in New York to a store in Dallas, Texas, are shipped "F.O.B.   16.____
    St. Louis, Missouri." The point at which title passes is the

    A. New York City R.R. depot
    B. Dallas, Texas R.R. depot
    C. St. Louis R.R. depot
    D. store in Dallas

17. If the time allowed for payment of a bill runs from the date of the invoice, the terms of sale   17.____
    are made under what is called

    A. advance dating   B. R.O.G. dating
    C. E.O.M. dating   D. ordinary dating

18. An extra discount allowed by vendors when a bill is paid before the expiration of the cash   18.____
    discount period is called

    A. anticipation   B. trade discount
    C. quantity discount   D. special discount

19. The expected period of time between ordering merchandise and its receipt into stock is known as the

    A. re-order period
    B. safety factor
    C. delivery period
    D. minimum stock period

20. The amount a buyer may spend on purchases is known as

    A. planned purchases
    B. open to buy
    C. commitments
    D. concentration of buying

21. The ratio between net sales and average inventory at cost is

    A. stock turn
    B. stock turn rate
    C. stock-sales ratio
    D. capital turnover

22. If goods are sold on May 1, terms 2/10 E.O.M., the net amount is due

    A. June 30   B. June 10   C. July 10   D. May 31

23. A sale of 500 pounds of oats from a crib containing 2500 pounds is an example of a

    A. divisible sale
    B. bulk sale
    C. sale of fungible goods
    D. sale of unique personal property

24. The traffic productivity ratio is

    A. transactions divided by traffic
    B. traffic divided by sales force
    C. traffic transactions divided by traffic
    D. units sold divided by traffic

25. "For deposit only, David Bernstein" is an example of the following type of endorsement:

    A. Blank
    B. Special
    C. Restrictive
    D. Qualified

26. The influence of changes in sales volume on profits caused by fixed expenses is known as

    A. commitments
    B. leverage
    C. retail reductions
    D. mark downs

27. The following defense would be valid against a holder in due course:

    A. Duress
    B. Infancy of maker
    C. Fraud in the inducement
    D. Non-delivery of the completed instrument

28. Variable expenses representing a specific dollar and cents cost for handling a single unit to merchandise is a(n)

    A. value variable expense
    B. flat expense
    C. fixed expense
    D. overhead expense

29. The sum of the beginning inventory and the purchases, less the final inventory, is known as 29.____

   A. total merchandise handled
   B. alteration costs
   C. cost of sales
   D. commitments

30. Barton issues a thirty-day note on May 1 and post-dates the note May 10. Barton dies on May 3. The payee should demand payment no later than 30.____

   A. May 31   B. June 9   C. May 3   D. June 2

KEY (CORRECT ANSWERS)

1.	D	11.	B	21.	D
2.	C	12.	C	22.	A
3.	A	13.	B	23.	C
4.	C	14.	B	24.	D
5.	B	15.	B	25.	C
6.	A	16.	C	26.	B
7.	B	17.	D	27.	B
8.	C	18.	A	28.	B
9.	C	19.	C	29.	C
10.	C	20.	B	30.	A

TEST 2

DIRECTIONS: Each question or incomplete statement is followed by several suggested answers or completions. Select the one that BEST answers the question or completes the statement. *PRINT THE LETTER OF THE CORRECT ANSWER IN THE SPACE AT THE RIGHT.*

1. Which of the following statements concerning the usual illumination of a store is INCORRECT?   1._____

   A. General interior – 50 to 75 foot candles
   B. Show cases – 50 to 100 foot candles
   C. Show windows – 60 to 200 foot candles
   D. None of these

2. A warranty deducible from conduct or circumstances is a(n)   2._____

   A. implied warranty   B. express warranty
   C. materiality   D. guaranty

3. The man in charge of store records and of setting and checking the standards of performance of the various departments is the   3._____

   A. auditor   B. merchandise manager
   C. personnel manager   D. controller

4. Hand-to-mouth buying by retailers takes place when   4._____

   A. prices are falling
   B. prices are rising
   C. prices are steady
   D. inflation is taking place

5. The maxim of "caveat emptor" applies when   5._____

   A. defects are latent
   B. defects are patent
   C. sale is made by sample
   D. sale is made by description

6. An executory sale is a   6._____

   A. contract of sale
   B. contract to sell
   C. sale of specific goods
   D. sale by the executor of an estate

7. The expense for interest charged at a standard rate on the major assets of a business is known as   7._____

   A. imputed interest   B. cash discounts lost
   C. bank discount   D. prepaid interest

8. The display of a completely outfitted kitchen is BEST described as a(n) 8.____

   A. open display
   B. closed display
   C. architectural display
   D. platform display

9. The transfer of title in one chattel for title in another is a 9.____

   A. sale B. gift C. barter D. bailment

10. If goods are sold by sample, title passes to the buyer when the 10.____

    A. contract is made
    B. goods are set aside by the seller for the buyer
    C. goods are paid out
    D. goods are delivered

11. The Progressive Grocer has reported that supermarkets and superettes are responsible 11.____
    for the following percentage of the total food business in the United States:

    A. Over 80 percent
    B. Over 90 percent
    C. Over 70 percent
    D. Over 60 percent

12. A customer is looking at ties, and the salesman says as he approaches, "These all silk 12.____
    ties will not wrinkle." This is an example of the type of approach known as the

    A. formal
    B. service
    C. psychological
    D. merchandise

13. An instrument is not negotiable if it is payable 13.____

    A. at 30 days' sight
    B. on demand
    C. 30 days after the death of the maker
    D. 30 days after the marriage of the maker

14. Placing the retail price on the duplicate purchase order is called 14.____

    A. coding
    B. pre-retailing
    C. invoicing
    D. billing

15. A negotiable instrument based on past consideration is 15.____

    A. unenforceable
    B. valid
    C. enforceable by holder in due course only
    D. unenforceable by payee if the maker sets up past consideration as a defense

16. A greeting that receives the general approval of skillful salespeople and satisfied custom- 16.____
    ers is:

    A. Good morning.
    B. Something in ties?
    C. Are you looking for something?
    D. Do you want anything?

17. William Whiteson, agent for Richard Barber, signs a note, "William Whiteson, Agent." A holder in due course can collect from

   A. Barber only
   B. Whiteson only
   C. Barber and Whiteson
   D. Either Barber or Whiteson, at the holder's election

18. Counting and listing merchandise received without reference to the invoice or order is called a

   A. direct check
   B. indirect check
   C. blind check
   D. cross check

19. An instrument does NOT need to be _____ in order to be negotiable.

   A. dated
   B. in writing
   C. signed by maker or drawer
   D. payable to order or to bearer

20. A form on which salespeople report customers' requests for merchandise which is not in stock is a

   A. purchase order
   B. want slip
   C. check list
   D. model stock list

21. In a sale of fungible goods, title passes to the buyer when the

   A. goods are delivered
   B. the contract is made
   C. goods are set aside by the seller for the buyer
   D. goods are paid for

22. When sales prices are quickly influenced by changes in replacement costs, the inventory method which is MOST appropriate is

   A. retail price
   B. average inventory
   C. fifo
   D. lifo

23. The United States Chamber of Commerce has estimated that discount firms account for the following percentage of the total retail sales in the nation:

   A. 5 percent
   B. 28 percent
   C. 18 percent
   D. 35 percent

24. An excellent source of merchandise with which a retailer concentrates a considerable portion of his buying is known as a

   A. central buying office
   B. group buying office
   C. key resource
   D. direct buying office

25. If goods are sold F.O.B. Destination, title passes to the buyer when the

   A. goods are delivered to the buyer
   B. goods are delivered to the carrier
   C. contract is made
   D. goods are paid for

26. A carrier is not obligated to honor a seller's right of stoppage in transit if   26.____

   A. goods are sold on credit
   B. goods are still in transit
   C. carrier has issued an order bill of lading
   D. the buyer is insolvent

27. If goods are sold "with privilege of return," title passes to the buyer when   27.____

   A. the goods are delivered
   B. the buyer indicates his approval by words or action
   C. the contract is made
   D. the goods are paid for

28. An additional bonus paid to salespeople for pushing certain items usually of a slow-selling nature is referred to as a(n)   28.____

   A. X.B.   B. P.M.   C. A.M.   D. X.X.

29. A seller has a possessory lien if he has   29.____

   A. title and possession
   B. possession but not title
   C. title but not possession
   D. neither title nor possession

30. Low-priced articles frequently purchased by customers with a minimum of effort, and without making comparisons, are known as   30.____

   A. fashion goods   B. convenience goods
   C. shopping goods   D. loss leaders

KEY (CORRECT ANSWERS)

1.	A	11.	A	21.	B
2.	A	12.	D	22.	D
3.	D	13.	D	23.	C
4.	A	14.	B	24.	C
5.	B	15.	B	25.	A
6.	B	16.	A	26.	C
7.	A	17.	B	27.	A
8.	C	18.	C	28.	B
9.	C	19.	A	29.	B
10.	B	20.	B	30.	B

INTERPRETING STATISTICAL DATA GRAPHS, CHARTS AND TABLES
EXAMINATION SECTION
TEST 1

DIRECTIONS: Each question or incomplete statement is followed by several suggested answers or completions. Select the one that BEST answers the question or completes the statement. *PRINT THE LETTER OF THE CORRECT ANSWER IN THE SPACE AT THE RIGHT.*

Questions 1-5.

DIRECTIONS: Questions 1 through 5 are to be answered SOLELY on the basis of the information given below.

	LISTING OF PAPER, 100% SULPHITE, FOUND IN STOCKROOM A			
Description	Quantity Ordered by Stockroom A (In dozen reams)	Quantity in Stock Before Delivery (In dozen reams)	Cost Per Ream	Location of Stock in Stockroom
8 1/2"x11" Blue	17	5	$1.88	Bin A7
8 1/2"x11" Buff	8	3	$1.86	Bin A7
8 1/2"x11" Green	11	4	$1.90	Bin B4
8 1/2"x11" Pink	10	4	$1.86	Bin B4
8 1/2"x11" White	80	15	$1.72	Bin A8
8 1/2"x13" White	76	12	$2.04	Bin A8
8 1/2"x14" Blue	7	2	$2.38	Bin A7
8 1/2"x14" Buff	7	3	$2.36	Bin A7
8 1/2"x14" Green	5	2	$2.40	Bin B4
8 1/2"x14" Pink	8	4	$2.36	Bin B4
8 1/2"x14" White	110	28	$2.30	Bin A8
81/2"x14" Yellow	2	1	$2.46	Bin C6

1. How many reams of 8 1/2" x 13" paper will there be in stock if only one-half of the amount ordered is delivered? _____ reams.   1._____

   A. 456   B. 600   C. 912   D. 1,056

2. Suppose all ordered material is delivered.   2._____
   The bin that will have the MOST reams of paper is

   A. A7   B. A8   C. B4   D. C6

37

2 (#1)

3. Suppose all ordered material has been delivered. What is the APPROXIMATE value of all 8 1/2" x 11" paper which is in Bin B4?

   A. $54   B. $342   C. $396   D. $654

4. How many reams of white paper of all sizes were ordered?
   _____ reams.

   A. 55   B. 266   C. 660   D. 3,192

5. Before any of the orders were delivered, the following requests were filled and removed from the stockroom:
   2 dozen reams 8 1/2" x 11" Blue; 2 dozen reams 8 1/2" x 11" Green; 7 dozen reams 8 1/2" x 11" White; 5 dozen reams 8 1/2" x 13" White; 1 dozen reams 8 1/2" x 14" Green; 13 dozen reams 8 1/2" x 14" White.
   How many reams of paper were left in the stockroom after the above requests were filled?

   A. 30   B. 53   C. 636   D. 996

KEY (CORRECT ANSWERS)

1. B
2. B
3. D
4. D
5. C

TEST 2

Questions 1-4.

DIRECTIONS: Questions 1 through 4 are to be answered SOLELY on the basis of the information given below.

> NUMBER OF SPECIAL ORDERS PICKED AND PACKED EACH DAY DURING WEEK
> Stockman A - Monday 20; Tuesday 20; Wednesday. 25;
> Thursday. 30; Friday 30
> Stockman B - Monday 25; Tuesday 30; Wednesday 35;
> Thursday 20; Friday 35
> Stockman C - Monday 15; Tuesday 20; Wednesday 25;
> Thursday 30; Friday 30
> Stockman D - Monday 30; Tuesday 35; Wednesday 40;
> Thursday 35; Friday 40

1. Which stockman picked and packed a total of exactly 120 special orders during the week?
   Stockman

   A. A   B. B   C. C   D. D

2. The stockman who picked and packed the LEAST number of special orders on Thursday is Stockman

   A. A   B. B   C. C   D. D

3. The total number of special orders picked and packed during the week by all four stockmen is

   A. 125   B. 460   C. 560   D. 570

4. By what percentage did the number of orders picked and packed by Stockman C on Friday exceed the number of orders picked and packed by Stockman C on Monday?

   A. 15%   B. 30%   C. 100%   D. 200%

KEY (CORRECT ANSWERS)

1. C
2. B
3. D
4. C

TEST 3

Questions 1-6.

DIRECTIONS: Questions 1 through 6 are to be answered SOLELY on the basis of the information given in the table below.

RECORD OF INCOMING FREIGHT SHIPMENTS

Date Received	Purchase Order No.	Prepaid	Amount To Be Collected	Shipper	No. of Items	Weight	Shippers' Catalog No.
1/7	9616	$15.10		Harding Grove Equip.	14	170	28
1/12	3388		$ 2.00	People's Paper, Inc.	10	50	091
1/12	8333		$106.19	Falls Office Supply	25	2,500	701
2/2	7126		$ 9.00	Leigh Foods	175	4,000	47
2/13	4964		$ 3.09	McBride Paper Co.	14	75	83
4/13	3380	$14.09		Central Hardware	14	1,750	019
4/30	7261		$ 6.90	Northwestern Foods	121	2,100	13
5/12	9166	$10.50		Harding Grove Equipment	15	50	36
5/17	6949		$ 4.19	Black's Paper Co.	40	65	743
5/31	6691		$ 20.00	Central Hardware	16	600	563
6/30	5388	$ 9.75		Harding Grove Equip.	15	15	420
6/30	8308		$ 22.50	Falls Office Supply	19	290	97
8/23	8553		$ 4.90	Tremont Paper, Inc.	75	570	36
9/12	5338	$ 6.91		Northeast Hardware	51	901	071
10/15	6196	$12.00		Mobray Hardware	60	786	131

1. What is the purchase order number for the Harding Grove equipment shipment that was received on 5/12?

   A. 9166   B. 5388   C. 9616   D. 6691

2. All items that cost less than five dollars ($5.00) came from shippers of

   A. paper   B. foods
   C. hardware   D. office supplies

40

2 (#3)

3. All items listed in the above table were delivered by   3.____

    A. U.S. Mail   B. freight
    C. air express   D. ship

4. On what date was the LARGEST number of items received?   4.____

    A. 2/2   B. 2/13   C. 4/30   D. 5/17

5. If all items shipped by Falls Office Supply on 1/12 were of equal weight, how much did each item weigh? _____ lbs.   5.____

    A. 10   B. 25   C. 100   D. 250

6. If the names of the shippers were put in alphabetical order, which of the following should be put AFTER McBride Paper Company?   6.____

    A. Northeast Hardware   B. Leigh Foods
    C. Northwestern Foods   D. Mobray Hardware

KEY (CORRECT ANSWERS)

1. A
2. A
3. B
4. A
5. C
6. D

TEST 4

Questions 1-6.

DIRECTIONS: Questions 1 through 6 are to be answered SOLELY on the basis of the information contained in the chart below, which shows the number of requisitions filled by Storeroom A during each month of 2018.

NUMBER OF REQUISITIONS HANDLED EACH MONTH
DURING 2018 BY STOREROOM A

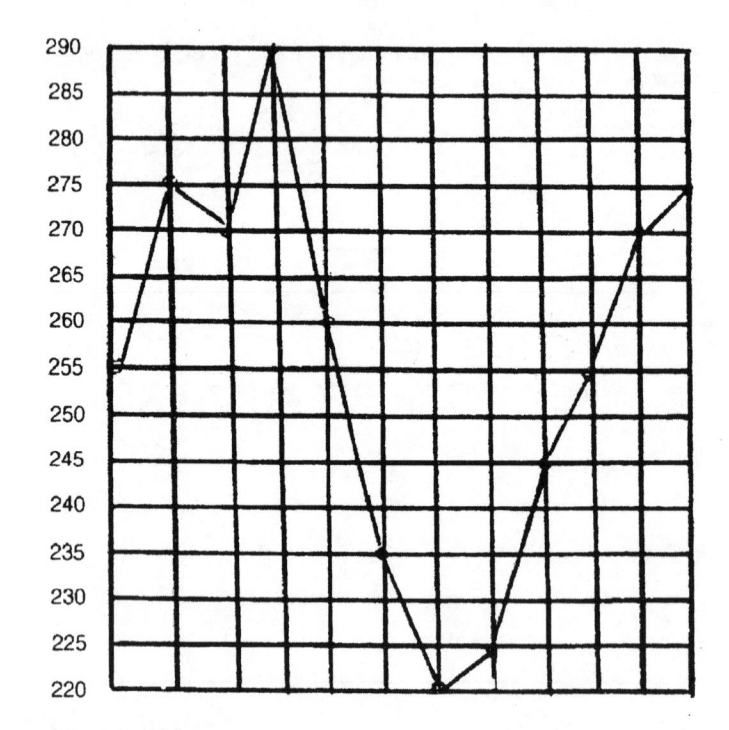

1. According to the above chart, the average number of requisitions handled per month by Storeroom A during the first six months is MOST NEARLY

   A. 250   B. 260   C. 270   D. 280

2. It is expected that the number of requisitions Storeroom A will handle in 2019 will be 10 percent more than it handled in 2018.
   The number of requisitions Storeroom A is expected to handle during the year is

   A. 2,763   B. 3,070   C. 3,377   D. 3,440

3. The month during which the number of requisitions handled showed the GREATEST decrease from the previous month was

   A. April   B. May   C. June   D. July

4. During May, there were 3 clerks assigned to Storeroom A. One man went on vacation for the month of June and was not replaced.
   The number of additional orders handled by each man working in June over the number of orders handled per man in May was MOST NEARLY

   A. 20 B. 27 C. 32 D. 36

5. During June, July, and August, 8 percent of the requisitions handled were rush orders. The number of rush orders handled during these three months is MOST NEARLY

   A. 55 B. 60 C. 65 D. 70

6. During November, there were three clerks assigned to Storeroom A.
   If one handled 95 requisitions and another handled 85 requisitions, the number of requisitions handled by the third clerk was

   A. 70 B. 80 C. 90 D. 100

KEY (CORRECT ANSWERS)

1. B
2. C
3. B
4. C
5. A
6. C

TEST 5

Questions 1-10.

DIRECTIONS: Questions 1 through 10 are to be answered SOLELY on the basis of the information given in the table below.

TABLE OF INFORMATION ABOUT GARDEN HOSE ON HAND

Commodity Index Number	Kind & Diameter of Hose (in inches)	Number of Feet Per Roll	Weight Per Roll lbs.	Weight Per Roll ozs.	Cost Per Roll	Number of Rolls on Hand
SL 14171	Plastic, 3/4"	25	6	5	$ 5.90	20
SL 14172	Plastic, 3/4"	50	12	5	9.90	50
SL 14271	Plastic, 5/8"	25	4	7	4.40	40
SL 14272	Plastic, 5/8"	50	8	10	7.40	50
SL 14273	Plastic, 5/8"	75	13	0	10.40	50
SL 14274	Plastic, 5/8"	100	17	0	13.40	100
SL 24171	Rubber, Reinforced, 3/4"	25	9	3	8.90	20
SL 24172	Rubber, Reinforced, 3/4"	50	18	0	14.90	10
SL 24271	Rubber, Reinforced, 5/8"	25	6	2	6.20	40
SL 24272	Rubber, Reinforced, 5/8"	50	12	2	10.90	40
SL 24273	Rubber, Reinforced, 5/8"	75	18	0	15.20	60
SL 24274	Rubber, Reinforced, 5/8"	100	24	0	19.90	100

1. The total number of 25 foot rolls of all types of garden hose currently on hand is

   A. 120   B. 180   C. 220   D. 400

   1.____

2. The total weight of one roll each of SL 14172, SL 14273, SL 24271, and SL 24274 is _____ lbs. _____ oz.

   A. 49; 7   B. 51; 7   C. 55; 7   D. 61; 7

   2.____

3. The total weight of all of the 25 foot rolls of rubber, reinforced, 5/8" garden hose on hand is _____ lbs.

   A. 175   B. 240   C. 245   D. 485

   3.____

4. An order for 10 rolls of SL 14271, 17 rolls of SL 14274, and 22 rolls of SL 24271 will MOST NEARLY weigh _____ lbs.

   A. 333   B. 423   C. 468   D. 472

   4.____

5. The total cost of 12 rolls of 100 foot plastic, 5/8" garden hose is

   A. $124.80   B. $134.00   C. $160.80   D. $238.80

   5.____

44

6. Assume that from the 40 rolls of SL 24272 and the 100 rolls of SL 24274 you ship one order of 10 rolls of SL 24272 and one order of 50 rolls of SL 24274.
   The total cost of all of the SL 24272 and the SL 24274 garden hose still on hand after filling these orders is

   A. $479 B. $1,104 C. $1,322 D. $1,451

7. Assume that 15% of all the 100 foot rolls of plastic garden hose and rubber reinforced garden hose are found defective.
   Then, the total cost of the defective hose is

   A. $199.00 B. $298.00 C. $333.00 D. $499.50

8. The stock on hand of which one of the following sizes and types of garden hose has the GREATEST total cost?

   A. SL 14171 B. SL 14271 C. SL 24171 D. SL 24172

9. If 3/4" plastic garden hose is taken from the 50 foot rolls, then the cost of one foot of such hose is MOST NEARLY

   A. 20¢ B. 23¢ C. 26¢ D. 29¢

10. If it takes one worker one hour to inspect 20 rolls of garden hose for defects, the LEAST amount of time it will take two workers to inspect ALL the rolls of garden hose in stock is _____ hours _____ minutes.

    A. 14; 30 B. 15; 50 C. 24; 10 D. 29; 0

KEY (CORRECT ANSWERS)

1. A   6. C
2. C   7. D
3. C   8. C
4. C   9. A
5. C   10. A

READING COMPREHENSION
UNDERSTANDING AND INTERPRETING WRITTEN MATERIAL
EXAMINATION SECTION
TEST 1

DIRECTIONS: Each question or incomplete statement is followed by several suggested answers or completions. Select the one that BEST answers the question or completes the statement. *PRINT THE LETTER OF THE CORRECT ANSWER IN THE SPACE AT THE RIGHT.*

Questions 1-10.

DIRECTIONS: Questions 1 through 10 are to be answered SOLELY on the basis of the DESCRIPTION OF ACCIDENT given below.

DESCRIPTION OF ACCIDENT

On Friday, May 9th, at about 2:30 P.M., Bus Operator Joe Able, Badge No. 1234, was operating his half-filled bus, Authority No. 5678, northbound along Fifth Ave. when a green Ford truck, N.Y. License No. 9012, driven by Sam Wood, came out of an Authority storeroom entrance into the path of the bus. To avoid hitting the truck, Joe Able turned his steering wheel sharply to the left, causing his bus to cross the solid white line into the opposite lane where the bus crashed head-on into a black 1995 Mercury, N.Y. License No. 3456, driven by Bill Green. The crash caused the Mercury to sideswipe a blue VW, N.J. License No. 7890, driven by Jim White, which was double-parked while he made a delivery. The sudden movement of the bus caused one of the passengers, Mrs. Jane Smith, to fall, striking her head on one of the seats. Joe Able blew his horn vigorously to summon aid, and Security Officer Fred Norton, Badge No. 9876, and Stockman A1 Blue, Badge No. 5432, came out of the storeroom and rendered assistance. While Norton gave Mrs. Smith first aid, Blue summoned an ambulance for Green. A tow truck removed Green's car, and Able found that the bus could operate under its own power, so he returned to the garage.

1. The Ford truck was driven by
   A. Able   B. Green   C. Wood   D. White

2. The Authority No. of the bus was
   A. 1234   B. 5678   C. 9012   D. 3456

3. The bus was driven by
   A. Able   B. Green   C. Wood   D. White

4. The license number of the VW was
   A. 9012   B. 3456   C. 7890   D. 5432

5. The horn of the bus summoned
   A. Blue   B. Green   C. White   D. Smith

1.____

2.____

3.____

4.____

5.____

6. The badge number of the security officer was 6.____
   A. 5432   B. 5678   C. 1234   D. 9876

7. The Mercury was driven by 7.____
   A. Smith   B. Norton   C. White   D. Green

8. The bus was traveling 8.____
   A. north   B. east   C. south   D. west

9. The vehicle towed away was a 9.____
   A. bus   B. Ford   C. Mercury   D. VW

10. Mrs. Smith hurt her 10.____
    A. head   B. back   C. arm   D. leg

Questions 11-12.

DIRECTIONS: Questions 11 and 12 are to be answered SOLELY on the basis of the following paragraph.

The City Charter requires that all purchases be made according to definite standards, or specifications. A specification may be defined as a statement of particulars descriptive of materials, or performance, or both; or, as a description of the technical details of a required commodity or service; or as a statement of what the buyer wants the seller to furnish. The specification should concisely define the quality of the commodity that is required to meet the needs of the using agency but still provide as wide competition in sources of supply as possible. To be of maximum value, the specification should describe the commodity clearly and in sufficient detail to ensure obtaining the exact commodity required.

11. Suppose that a buyer prepared the following specification for an item: cotton, absorbent, rolled. 11.____
    Based on the information given in the above passage, this specification would NOT be of value MAINLY because the

    A. quality of cotton required is not described
    B. description is not concise
    C. mode of packaging is not stated
    D. using agency is not referred to

12. Based on the information given in the above passage, the MOST important indication that a specification has been well prepared is that the 12.____

    A. buyer gets few bids on the commodity
    B. commodity obtained meets the needs of the using agency
    C. commodity is procured at the lowest possible cost
    D. commodity is described in great detail

Questions 13-15.

DIRECTIONS: Questions 13 through 15 are to be answered SOLELY on the basis of the following paragraph.

    The receiving department should inspect the exterior condition of the packaging when a shipment is received before signing the dray ticket. When it is obvious that the package has been broken or dropped and there is apparent damage, this fact should be noted on such dray ticket. A clear receipt should not be given the carrier's representative unless the package, to all outward appearances, is undamaged. If the package is received in an undamaged condition and at a later date it is discovered that the material within the package is damaged, such concealed damage still gives the receiver an opportunity to make claim against the transportation company. However, a claim of concealed damage is more difficult to substantiate. When concealed damage is discovered, the carrier should be notified promptly of this fact by telephone, and a claim as well as a request for inspection should be made. Carriers usually insist that all packaging materials and cartons be retained by the receiving department until this inspection has been made by the carrier. Should the carrier decline the opportunity to inspect the damaged shipment, he merely informs the receiving department to go ahead and proceed with filing a claim. A claim number should be obtained when making such telephone call.

13. Of the following, the MOST suitable title for the foregoing passage is

    A. ACCEPTANCE OF MATERIAL UPON RECEIPT
    B. ESSENTIALS OF PROPER PACKAGING
    C. PROCEDURE FOR RETURNING DAMAGED MERCHANDISE
    D. THE IMPORTANCE OF THE DRAY TICKET IN SECURING COMPENSATION FOR DAMAGES

14. Of the following, the BEST evidence that the carrier had been notified of the existence of concealed damage would *probably* be the

    A. claim number
    B. defective merchandise
    C. dray ticket
    D. packaging materials if defective

15. Of the following, the MOST likely reason for the carrier's insistence that packaging materials be retained in the event of concealed damage until the carrier has made the inspection is that the carrier may

    A. be able to advise the supplier of the need to be more careful in the future in the selection of packaging materials
    B. be better able to train his employees in more efficient materials handling techniques
    C. have evidence in the event of an action by the carrier against the supplier
    D. utilize the same packaging materials in returning the defective merchandise to the supplier

Questions 16-18.

DIRECTIONS: Questions 16 through 18 are to be answered SOLELY on the basis of the following paragraphs.

The use of a recognized brand name to describe a need is a method familiar to school purchasing officials. This is a simple though not always satisfactory ordering description. It has the advantage of being more readily understood by the supplier, and the buyer can be assured of obtaining the desired manufacturer's product. The difficulty of attempting to express specific physical or chemical requirements is eliminated by accepting the manufacturer's formula. User acceptance may be more readily obtained because an established and familiar product is procured. A disadvantage of this method is that it eliminates competition at the manufacturer's level.

A purchasing agent often has the feeling that unless he makes complete use of purchase specifications, he is not doing an adequate buying job. Nothing is further from the truth. The other methods of describing quality are often used by the practicing purchasing agent. Not all requirements can be reduced to specific terms. Small purchases, of which schools have many, are not economically acquired by the use of purchase specifications because of the cost of preparing such specifications. It must also be remembered that when the purchaser does buy by specifications, he assumes responsibility for the performance of the product he specifies, since he has drawn the rules of how it is to be made and what its composition will be. Wise selection of the method of describing quality is perhaps a more essential prerequisite for a purchasing agent than the ability to prepare purchase specifications for each item he buys.

16. Of the following, the MOST suitable title for the foregoing passage would be

    A. ADVANTAGES OF BUYING BY SPECIFICATION
    B. BUYING IN SMALL QUANTITIES
    C. METHODS OF PURCHASING
    D. PREPARING THE PURCHASE SPECIFICATION

17. An advantage of buying by the use of a purchase specification implied by the author is that

    A. brand name merchandise is more likely to carry a warranty
    B. certain purchasing requirements cannot be expressed in writing with a high degree of precision
    C. it often enables purchasing in quantity at a lower cost based on specific needs
    D. purchase specifications can readily be prepared

18. According to the foregoing passage, an advantage of purchasing by brand name implied by the author is that

    A. brand name merchandise is nearly always more suited for long-term usage than unbranded merchandise
    B. it encourages bidding by manufacturers of like products
    C. manufacturers of brand name preparations change the formulas of their products
    D. persons generally prefer using a well-known item

Questions 19-24.

DIRECTIONS: Questions 19 through 24 are to be answered SOLELY on the basis of the following paragraph on THEFT.

THEFT

A security officer must be alert at all times to discourage the willful removal of property and material of the Authority by individuals for self gain. Should a security officer detect such an individual, he should detain him and immediately call the supervisor at that location. No force should be used during the process of detainment. However, should the individual bolt from the premises, the security officer will be expected to offer some clues for his apprehension. Therefore, he should try to remember some characteristic traits about the individual, such as clothing, height, coloring, speech, and how he made his approach. Unusual characteristics, such as a scar or a limp, are most important. If a car is used, the security officer should take the license plate number of said car. Above information should be supplied to the responding peace officer and the special inspection control desk. In desolate locations, the security officer should first call the police and then the special inspection control desk. Any security officer having information of the theft should contact the director of special inspection by telephone or by mail. This information will be kept confidential if desired.

19. A security officer is required to be attentive on the job at all times MAINLY to

    A. get as much work done as possible
    B. prevent the stealing of Authority property
    C. show his supervisor that he is doing a good job
    D. prevent any other security officer from patrolling the area to which he is assigned

20. In the second sentence, the word *detain* means MOST NEARLY

    A. delay   B. avoid   C. call   D. report

21. The prescribed course of action a security officer should take when he discovers a person stealing Authority property is to

    A. make sure that all gates are closed to prevent the thief from escaping
    B. detain the thief and quickly call the supervisor
    C. use his club to keep the thief there until the police arrive
    D. call another security officer for assistance

22. The MOST useful of the following descriptions of a runaway thief would be that he is a

    A. tall man who runs fast   B. man with blue eyes
    C. man with black hair   D. tall man who limps

23. The license plate number of a car which is used by a thief to escape should be reported by a security officer to the responding peace officer and the

    A. director of protection agents
    B. security officer's supervisor
    C. special inspection control desk
    D. department of motor vehicles

24. A security officer patrolling a desolate area has spotted a thief. The security officer should FIRST call 24._____

    A. his supervisor
    B. the police
    C. the special inspection control desk
    D. the director of special inspection

Questions 25-30.

DIRECTIONS: Questions 25 through 30 are to be answered SOLELY on the basis of the following paragraph on REGISTRY SHEETS.

REGISTRY SHEETS

Where registry sheets are in effect, the security officer must legibly print Authority employee's pass number, title, license and vehicle number, destination, time in and time out; and each Authority employee must sign his or her name. The same procedure is to be applied to visitors, except in place of a pass number each visitor will indicate his address or firm name; and visitors must also sign waivers. Information is to be obtained from driver's license, firm credential card, or any other appropriate identification. All visitors must state their purpose for entering upon the property. If they desire to visit anyone, verification must be made before entry is permitted. All persons signing sheet must sign in when entering upon the property, and sign out again when leaving. The security officer will, at the end of his tour, draw a horizontal line across the entire sheet after his last entry, indicating the end of one tour and the beginning of another. At the top of each sheet, the security officer will enter the number of entries made during his tour, the sheet number, post, and date. Sheets are to begin with number 1 on the first day of the month and should be kept in numerical order. Each security officer will read the orders at each post to see whether any changes are made and at which hours control sheets are in effect.

25. Waivers need NOT be signed by 25._____

    A. Authority employees   B. vendors
    C. reporters   D. salesmen

26. All visitors are required to state 26._____

    A. whether they have a criminal record
    B. the reason for their visit
    C. the reason they are not bonded
    D. whether they have ever worked for the Authority

27. In the paragraph, the statement is made that *verification must be made before entry is permitted.* 27._____
The word *verification* means MOST NEARLY

    A. allowance   B. confirmation
    C. refusal   D. disposal

28. A security officer must draw a horizontal line across the entire registry sheet in order to show that   28._____

    A. he is being replaced to check a disturbance outside
    B. the last tour for the day has been completed
    C. one tour is ending and another is beginning
    D. a visitor has finished his business and is leaving

29. At the top of a registry sheet, it is NOT necessary for a security officer to list the   29._____

    A. tour number   B. number of entries made
    C. sheet number   D. date

30. A security officer should check at which hours control sheets are in effect by reading   30._____

    A. registry sheet number 1 on the first day of each month
    B. the orders at each post
    C. the time in and time out that each person has entered on the registry sheet
    D. the last entry made on the registry sheet used before the start of his tour

KEY (CORRECT ANSWERS)

1.	C	16.	C
2.	B	17.	C
3.	A	18.	D
4.	C	19.	B
5.	A	20.	A
6.	D	21.	B
7.	D	22.	D
8.	A	23.	C
9.	C	24.	B
10.	A	25.	A
11.	A	26.	B
12.	B	27.	B
13.	A	28.	C
14.	A	29.	A
15.	C	30.	B

TEST 2

DIRECTIONS: Each question or incomplete statement is followed by several suggested answers or completions. Select the one that BEST answers the question or completes the statement. *PRINT THE LETTER OF THE CORRECT ANSWER IN THE SPACE AT THE RIGHT.*

Questions 1-4.

DIRECTIONS: Questions 1 through 4 are to be answered using ONLY the information in the following passage.

    The operation and maintenance of the stock-location system is a warehousing function and responsibility. The stock locator system shall consist of a file of stock-location record cards, either manually or mechanically prepared, depending upon the equipment available. The file shall contain an individual card for each stock item stored in the depot, with the records maintained in stock number sequence.

    The locator file is used for all receiving, warehousing, inventory, and shipping activities in the depot. The locator file must contain complete and accurate data to provide ready support to the various depot functions and activities, i.e., processing shipping documents, updating records on mechanized equipment, where applicable, supplying accurate locator information for stock selection and proper storage of receipts, consolidating storage locations of identical items not subject to shelf-life control, and preventing the consolidation of stock of limited shelf-life items. The file is also essential in accomplishing location surveys and the inventory program.

    Storage of bulk stock items by *spot location* method is generally recognized as the best means of obtaining maximum warehouse space utilization. Despite the fact that the spot-location method of storage enables full utilization of storage capacity, this method may prove inefficient unless it is supplemented by adequate stock-location control, including proper lay-out and accurate maintenance of stock locator cards.

1. The manner in which the stock-location record cards should be filed is

    A. alphabetically   B. chronologically
    C. numerically   D. randomly

2. Items of limited shelf-life should

    A. not be stored
    B. not be stored together
    C. be stored in stock sequence
    D. be stored together

3. Which one of the following is NOT mentioned in the passage as a use of the stock-location system? Aids in

    A. accomplishing location surveys
    B. providing information for stock selection
    C. storing items received for the first time
    D. processing shipping documents

4. If the spot-location method of storing is used, then the use of the stock-location system is   4.____

   A. *desirable because* the stock-location system is recognized as the best means of obtaining maximum warehouse space utilization
   B. *undesirable* because additional records must be kept
   C. *desirable because* stock-location controls are necessary with the spot-location storage method
   D. *undesirable* because a stock-locator system will take up valuable storage space

Questions 5-8.

DIRECTIONS: Questions 5 through 8 are to be answered using ONLY the information in the following paragraph.

   Known damage is defined as damage that is apparent and acknowledged by the carrier at the time of delivery to the purchaser. A meticulous inspection of the damaged goods should be completed by the purchaser, and a notation specifying the extent of the damage should be applied to the carrier's original freight bill. As is the case in known loss, it is necessary for the carrier's agent to acknowledge by signature the damage notation in order for it to have any legal status. The purchaser should not refuse damaged freight since it is his legal duty to accept the property and to employ every available and reasonable means to protect the shipment and minimize the loss. Acceptance of a damaged shipment does not endanger any legitimate claim the purchaser may have against the carrier for damage. If the purchaser fails to observe the legal duty to accept damaged freight, the carrier may consider it abandoned. After properly notifying the vendor and purchaser of his intentions, the carrier may dispose of the material at public sale.

5. Before disposing of an abandoned shipment, the carrier must   5.____

   A. notify the vendor and the carrier's agent
   B. advise the vendor and purchaser of his plans
   C. notify the purchaser and the carrier's agent
   D. obtain the signature of the carrier's agent on the freight bill

6. In the case of damaged freight, the original freight bill will only have legal value if it is signed by the   6.____

   A. carrier's agent   B. purchaser
   C. vendor   D. purchaser and vendor

7. A purchaser does not protect a shipment of cargo that is damaged and is further deteriorating.   7.____
   According to the above paragraph, the action of the purchaser is

   A. *acceptable* because he is not obligated to protect damaged cargo
   B. *unacceptable* because damaged cargo must be protected no matter what is involved
   C. *acceptable* because he took possession of the cargo
   D. *unacceptable* because he is obligated by law to protect the cargo

8. The TWO requirements that must be satisfied before cargo can be labeled *known damage* are signs of evident damage and

   A. confirmation by the carrier or carrier's agent that this is so
   B. delayed shipment of goods
   C. signature of acceptance by the purchaser
   D. acknowledgment by the vendor that this is so

8.____

9. A hundred years ago, the steamboat was the center of life in the thriving Mississippi towns. Came the railroads; river traffic dwindled, and the white-painted vessels rotted at the wharves. During the World War, the government decided to relieve rail congestion by reviving the long-forgotten waterways.
According to the above paragraph,

   A. the railroads were once the center of thriving river towns on the Mississippi River
   B. the volume of river transportation was greater than the volume of rail transportation during the World War
   C. business found river transportation more profitable than railroad transportation during the World War
   D. in the past century the volume of transportation on the Mississippi River has varied

9.____

Questions 10-13.

DIRECTIONS: Questions 10 through 13 are to be answered ONLY on the basis of the following paragraph.

Several special factors must be taken into account in selecting trucks to be used in a warehouse that stores food in freezer and cold storage rooms. Since gasoline fumes may contaminate the food, the trucks should be powered by electricity, not by gasoline. The trucks must be specially equipped to operate in the extreme cold of freezer rooms. The equipment must be dependable, for if a truck breaks down while transporting frozen food from a railroad car to the freezer or a warehouse, this expensive merchandise will quickly spoil. Finally, since cold storage and freezer rooms are expensive to operate, commodities must be stored close together, and the aisles between the rows of commodities must be as narrow as possible. Therefore, the trucks must be designed to work even in narrow aisles.

10. Of the following, the BEST title for the above passage is

    A. EXPENSES INVOLVED IN OPERATING A FREEZER OR COLD STORAGE ROOM
    B. HOW TO PREVENT FOOD SPOILAGE IN FREEZER AND COLD STORAGE ROOMS
    C. SELECTING THE BEST TRUCKS TO USE IN A FOOD STORAGE WAREHOUSE
    D. THE PROBLEM OF CONTAMINATION OF FOOD BY GASOLINE FUMES

10.____

11. According to the above passage, electrically powered trucks should be used for moving food in freezer and cold storage rooms CHIEFLY because they

    A. are cheaper to operate than gasoline powered trucks
    B. are dependable

11.____

C. can operate in extremes of heat and cold
D. do not produce fumes which may contaminate food

12. Trucks designed for use in narrow aisles should be used in freezer and cold storage rooms because

    A. commodities are placed close together in freezer rooms to save space
    B. commodities spoil quickly if the space between aisles in the freezer is too wide
    C. narrow aisle trucks are more dependable
    D. narrow aisle trucks are run by electricity

13. According to the above paragraph, all of the following factors should be taken into account in selecting a truck for use to transport frozen food into and within a cold storage room EXCEPT

    A. ability to operate in extreme cold
    B. dependability
    C. the weight of the truck
    D. whether or not the truck emits exhaust fumes

Questions 14-18.

DIRECTIONS: Questions 14 through 18 are to be answered ONLY on the basis of the information contained in the following passage.

Floors in warehouses, storerooms, and shipping rooms must be strong enough to stay level under heavy loads. Unevenness of floors may cause boxes of materials to topple and fall. Safe floor load capacities and maximum heights to which boxes may be stacked should be posted conspicuously so all can notice it. Where material in boxes, containers, or cartons of the same weight is regularly stored, it is good practice to paint a horizontal line on the wall indicating the maximum height to which the material may be piled. A qualified expert should determine floor load capacity from the building plans, the age and condition of the floor supports, the type of floor, and other related information.

Working aisles are those from which material is placed into and removed from storage. Working aisles are of two types: transportation aisles running the length of the building and cross aisles running across the width of the building. Deciding on the number, width, and location of working aisles is important. While aisles are necessary and determine boundaries of storage areas, they reduce the space actually used for storage.

14. According to the passage above, how should safe floor load capacities be made known to employees?
    They should be

    A. given out to each employee
    B. given to supervisors only
    C. printed in large red letters
    D. posted so that they are easily seen

15. According to the passage above, floor load capacities should be determined by

    A. warehouse supervisors   B. the fire department
    C. qualified experts   D. machine operators

16. According to the above passage, transportation aisles   16._____

    A. run the length of the building
    B. run across the width of the building
    C. are wider than cross aisles
    D. are shorter than cross aisles

17. According to the above passage, working aisles tend to   17._____

    A. take away space that could be used for storage
    B. add to space that could be used for storage
    C. slow down incoming stock
    D. speed up outgoing stock

18. According to the passage above, unevenness of floors may cause   18._____

    A. overall warehouse deterioration
    B. piles of stock to fall
    C. materials to spoil
    D. many worker injuries

Questions 19-22.

DIRECTIONS: Questions 19 through 22 are to be answered ONLY on the basis of the information contained in the following passage.

    Planning for the unloading of incoming trucks is not easy since generally little or no advance notice of truck arrivals is received. The height of the floor of truck bodies and loading platforms sometimes are different; this makes necessary the use of special unloading methods. When available, hydraulic ramps compensate for the differences in platform and truck floor levels. When hydraulic ramps are not available, forklift equipment can sometimes be used, if the truck springs are strong enough to support such equipment. In a situation like this, the unloading operation does not differ much from unloading a railroad boxcar. In the cases where the forklift truck or a hydraulic pallet jack cannot be used inside the truck, a pallet dolly should be placed inside the truck, so that the empty pallet can be loaded close to the truck contents and rolled easily to the truck door and platform.

19. According to the passage above, unloading trucks is   19._____

    A. easy to plan since the time of arrival is usually known beforehand
    B. the same as loading a railroad boxcar
    C. hard to plan since trucks arrive without notice
    D. a very normal thing to do

20. According to the above passage, which materials handling equipment can make up for the difference in platform and truck floor levels?   20._____

    A. Hydraulic jacks   B. Hydraulic ramps
    C. Forklift trucks   D. Conveyors

21. According to the passage above, what materials handling equipment can be used when a truck cannot support the weight of forklift equipment? 21.____

    A. A pallet dolly
    B. A hydraulic ramp
    C. Bridge plates
    D. A warehouse tractor

22. Which is the BEST title for the above passage? 22.____

    A. UNLOADING RAILROAD BOXCARS
    B. UNLOADING MOTOR TRUCKS
    C. LOADING RAIL BOXCARS
    D. LOADING MOTOR TRUCKS

Questions 23-26.

DIRECTIONS: Questions 23 through 26 are to be answered ONLY on the basis of the information given below.

Planning for storage layout in terms of the supplies to be stored involves the intelligent and realistic application of a stockman's basic resources — space. The main objective of storage planning is the maximum use of available space. The planning and layout of space are dependent upon the types of supplies expected to be stored, and certain characteristics must be considered. Some supplies must be protected from dampness, extreme changes of temperature, and other such conditions. Iron and steel products rust quickly at high temperatures with high humidity. High temperatures also cause some plastics to melt and change shape, while extreme dampness can cause paper to mildew and wood to warp. Hazardous articles, including flammable items like paint and rubber cement, should be stored separated from each other and from other types of supplies.

Extremes in characteristics such as size, shape, and weight need to be considered in laying out space. Large, awkward containers and unusually heavy items generally should be stored near doors with aisles leading directly to them and/or shipping and receiving facilities. Light and fragile items cannot be stacked to a height which would cause crushing or other damage to containers and contents. Fast-moving articles should be stored in locations from which they can be handled quickly and efficiently.

23. It is MOST important to store articles like paints and rubber cement in areas where 23.____

    A. they can be protected from theft
    B. shipping and receiving doors are easily accessible
    C. they can be isolated from other supplies
    D. boxes containing them can be stacked as high as possible

24. Storage locations from which items can be selected and issued quickly are recommended for supplies classified as 24.____

    A. fragile
    B. fast-moving
    C. under-sized
    D. flammable

25. In order to prevent supplies made of iron from rusting, they should be stored in areas with _____ humidity and _____ temperature.

   A. low; high
   B. low, low
   C. high; high
   D. high; low

26. Which of the following characteristics is NOT considered in the above passage on storage planning and layout?
   The _____ of the item to be stored.

   A. size
   B. quantity
   C. weight
   D. shape

Questions 27-30.

DIRECTIONS: Questions 27 through 30 are to be answered ONLY on the basis of the information given below.

The *active stock* portion of the inventory is that portion which is kept for the purpose of satisfying the shop's expected requirements of that material. It is directly related to the *order quantity*. The *order quantity* is found by determining the expected annual requirements of the shop and dividing this by the number of orders for this merchandise which will be placed during the year. The most economical number of orders is usually found by considering the cost of ordering and storing inventory.

The *safety stock* portion of the inventory is that portion which is created to take care of above-average or unexpected demands on the inventory. This portion is directly related to the point at which the order is placed. The amount of safety stock is not determined by comparing order costs and carrying costs, but on the need for protection against stock shortages for each stock item under consideration. Some stock items will need more safety stock than others, depending upon how much difference there has been in the past between the expected usage of material and the actual amount needed and used for any given time period, plus the reliability of the suppliers' delivery and of the order lead-time. If the expected usage of an item has always been 100% accurately predicted, then theoretically there would be no need for *safety stock*.

27. According to the above passage, the *active stock* inventory is that portion of the inventory which is

   A. used most frequently by management
   B. ordered on a regular basis, such as every month
   C. expected to meet the organization's anticipated inventory needs
   D. needed to protect against shortages in very active inventory items

28. According to the passage above, what factors must be considered to determine the order quantity for any active stock item?

   A. Anticipated requirements, ordering cost, and cost of storing inventory
   B. Order lead-time and delivery service
   C. Variety of stock items ordered in the previous year
   D. The largest quantity ever ordered

29. Maintaining a safety stock portion of the inventory is

    A. *good* because it provides for unexpected demands on the inventory
    B. *good* because it makes the inventory more valuable than it actually is
    C. *poor* because it provides unnecessary work for stockmen since the inventory is rarely used
    D. *poor* because it makes storage areas overcrowded and unsafe

30. The above passage indicates that 100 percent accuracy in forecasting future activity will eliminate the need for

    A. reliable deliveries
    B. active stock
    C. safety stock
    D. deviation in total order quantity

KEY (CORRECT ANSWERS)

1.	C		16.	A
2.	B		17.	A
3.	C		18.	B
4.	C		19.	C
5.	B		20.	B
6.	A		21.	A
7.	D		22.	B
8.	A		23.	C
9.	D		24.	B
10.	C		25.	B
11.	D		26.	B
12.	A		27.	C
13.	C		28.	A
14.	D		29.	A
15.	C		30.	C

PREPARING WRITTEN MATERIAL

EXAMINATION SECTION
TEST 1

DIRECTIONS: Each of the sentences in the tests that follow may be classified under one of the following four categories:

    A. *Incorrect* because of faulty grammar or sentence structure
    B. *Incorrect* because of faulty punctuation
    C. *Incorrect* because of faulty capitalization
    D. *Correct*

Examine each sentence carefully to determine under which of the above four options it is best classified. Then, in the space on the right, print the capital letter preceding the option which is the *BEST* of the four suggested above.

(Each incorrect sentence contains but one type of error. Consider a sentence to be correct if it contains none of the types of errors mentioned, even though there may be other correct ways of expressing the same thought.)

1. This fact, together with those brought out at the previous meeting, prove that the schedule is satisfactory to the employees.   1.____

2. Like many employees in scientific fields, the work of bookkeepers and accountants requires accuracy and neatness.   2.____

3. "What can I do for you," the secretary asked as she motioned to the visitor to take a seat.   3.____

4. Our representative, Mr. Charles will call on you next week to determine whether or not your claim has merit.   4.____

5. We expect you to return in the spring; please do not disappoint us.   5.____

6. Any supervisor, who disregards the just complaints of his subordinates, is remiss in the performance of his duty.   6.____

7. Because she took less than an hour for lunch is no reason for permitting her to leave before five o'clock.   7.____

8. "Miss Smith," said the supervisor, "Please arrange a meeting of the staff for two o'clock on Monday."   8.____

9. A private company's vacation and sick leave allowance usually differs considerably from a public agency.   9.____

10. Therefore, in order to increase the efficiency of operations in the department, a report on the recommended changes in procedures was presented to the departmental committee in charge of the program.   10.____

11. We told him to assign the work to whoever was available.   11.____

12. Since John was the most efficient of any other employee in the bureau, he received the highest service rating.   12.____

13. Only those members of the national organization who resided in the middle West attended the conference in Chicago.   13.____

14. The question of whether the office manager has as yet attained, or indeed can ever hope to secure professional status is one which has been discussed for years.   14.____

15. No one knew who to blame for the error which, we later discovered, resulted in a considerable loss of time.   15.____

KEY (CORRECT ANSWERS)

1.	A		6.	B
2.	A		7.	A
3.	B		8.	C
4.	B		9.	A
5.	D		10.	D

11. D
12. A
13. C
14. B
15. A

TEST 2

DIRECTIONS: Each of the sentences in the tests that follow may be classified under one of the following four categories:
- A. *Incorrect* because of faulty grammar or sentence structure
- B. *Incorrect* because of faulty punctuation
- C. *Incorrect* because of faulty capitalization
- D. *Correct*

1. The National alliance of Businessmen is trying to persuade private businesses to hire youth in the summertime.   1.____
2. The supervisor who is on vacation, is in charge of processing vouchers.   2.____
3. The activity of the committee at its conferences is always stimulating.   3.____
4. After checking the addresses again, the letters went to the mailroom.   4.____
5. The director, as well as the employees, are interested in sharing the dividends.   5.____

KEY (CORRECT ANSWERS)

1. C
2. B
3. D
4. A
5. A

TEST 3

DIRECTIONS: In each of the following groups of sentences, one of the four sentences is faulty in grammar, punctuation, or capitalization. Select the incorrect sentence in each case.

1. A. Sailing down the bay was a thrilling experience for me.
   B. He was not consulted about your joining the club.
   C. This story is different than the one I told you yesterday.
   D. There is no doubt about his being the best player.

   1.____

2. A. He maintains there is but one road to world peace.
   B. It is common knowledge that a child sees much he is not supposed to see.
   C. Much of the bitterness might have been avoided if arbitration had been resorted to earlier in the meeting.
   D. The man decided it would be advisable to marry a girl somewhat younger than him.

   2.____

3. A. In this book, the incident I liked least is where the hero tries to put out the forest fire.
   B. Learning a foreign language will undoubtedly give a person a better understanding of his mother tongue.
   C. His actions made us wonder what he planned to do next.
   D. Because of the war, we were unable to travel during the summer vacation.

   3.____

4. A. The class had no sooner become interested in the lesson than the dismissal bell rang.
   B. There is little agreement about the kind of world to be planned at the peace conference.
   C. "Today," said the teacher, "we shall read 'The Wind in the Willows.' I am sure you'll like it.
   D. The terms of the legal settlement of the family quarrel handicapped both sides for many years.

   4.____

5. A. I was so suprised that I was not able to say a word.
   B. She is taller than any other member of the class.
   C. It would be much more preferable if you were never seen in his company.
   D. We had no choice but to excuse her for being late.

   5.____

KEY (CORRECT ANSWERS)

1. C
2. D
3. A
4. C
5. C

TEST 4

DIRECTIONS: In each of the following groups of sentences, one of the four sentences is faulty in grammar, punctuation, or capitalization. Select the incorrect sentence in each case.

1. A. Please send me these data at the earliest opportunity.
   B. The loss of their material proved to be a severe handicap.
   C. My principal objection to this plan is that it is impracticable.
   D. The doll had laid in the rain for an hour and was ruined.

   1.____

2. A. The garden scissors, left out all night in the rain, were in a badly rusted condition.
   B. The girls felt bad about the misunderstanding which had arisen.
   C. Sitting near the campfire, the old man told John and I about many exciting adventures he had had.
   D. Neither of us is in a position to undertake a task of that magnitude.

   2.____

3. A. The general concluded that one of the three roads would lead to the besieged city.
   B. The children didn't, as a rule, do hardly anything beyond what they were told to do.
   C. The reason the girl gave for her negligence was that she had acted on the spur of the moment.
   D. The daffodils and tulips look beautiful in that blue vase.

   3.____

4. A. If I was ten years older, I should be interested in this work.
   B. Give the prize to whoever has drawn the best picture.
   C. When you have finished reading the book, take it back to the library.
   D. My drawing is as good as or better than yours.

   4.____

5. A. He asked me whether the substance was animal or vegetable.
   B. An apple which is unripe should not be eaten by a child.
   C. That was an insult to me who am your friend.
   D. Some spy must of reported the matter to the enemy.

   5.____

6. A. Limited time makes quoting the entire message impossible.
   B. Who did she say was going?
   C. The girls in your class have dressed more dolls this year than we.
   D. There was such a large amount of books on the floor that I couldn't find a place for my rocking chair.

   6.____

7. A. What with his sleeplessness and his ill health, he was unable to assume any responsibility for the success of the meeting.
   B. If I had been born in February, I should be celebrating my birthday soon.
   C. In order to prevent breakage, she placed a sheet of paper between each of the plates when she packed them.
   D. After the spring shower, the violets smelled very sweet.

   7.____

8. A. He had laid the book down very reluctantly before the end of the lesson.
   B. The dog, I am sorry to say, had lain on the bed all night.
   C. The cloth was first lain on a flat surface; then it was pressed with a hot iron.
   D. While we were in Florida, we lay in the sun until we were noticeably tanned.

   8.____

9. A. If John was in New York during the recent holiday season, I have no doubt he spent most of his time with his parents.
    B. How could he enjoy the television program; the dog was barking and the baby was crying.
    C. When the problem was explained to the class, he must have been asleep.
    D. She wished that her new dress were finished so that she could go to the party.

    9._____

10. A. The engine not only furnishes power but light and heat as well.
    B. You're aware that we've forgotten whose guilt was established, aren't you?
    C. Everybody knows that the woman made many sacrifices for her children.
    D. A man with his dog and gun is a familiar sight in this neighborhood.

    10._____

KEY (CORRECT ANSWERS)

1. D
2. C
3. B
4. A
5. D

6. D
7. B
8. C
9. B
10. A

TEST 5

DIRECTIONS: Each of Questions 1 to 15 consists of a sentence which may be classified appropriately under one of the following four categories:
A. *Incorrect* because of faulty grammar
B. *Incorrect* because of faulty punctuation
C. *Incorrect* because of faulty spelling
D. *Correct*

Examine each sentence carefully. Then, print, in the space on the right, the letter preceding the category which is the best of the four suggested above.

(Note: Each incorrect sentence contains only one type of error. Consider a sentence correct if it contains no errors, although there may be other correct ways of writing the sentence.)

1. Of the two employees, the one in our office is the most efficient. 1.____
2. No one can apply or even understand, the new rules and regulations. 2.____
3. A large amount of supplies were stored in the empty office. 3.____
4. If an employee is occassionally asked to work overtime, he should do so willingly. 4.____
5. It is true that the new procedures are difficult to use but, we are certain that you will learn them quickly. 5.____
6. The office manager said that he did not know who would be given a large allotment under the new plan. 6.____
7. It was at the supervisor's request that the clerk agreed to postpone his vacation. 7.____
8. We do not believe that it is necessary for both he and the clerk to attend the conference. 8.____
9. All employees, who display perseverance, will be given adequate recognition. 9.____
10. He regrets that some of us employees are dissatisfied with our new assignments. 10.____
11. "Do you think that the raise was merited," asked the supervisor? 11.____
12. The new manual of procedure is a valuable supplement to our rules and regulations. 12.____
13. The typist admitted that she had attempted to pursuade the other employees to assist her in her work. 13.____
14. The supervisor asked that all amendments to the regulations be handled by you and I. 14.____
15. The custodian seen the boy who broke the window. 15.____

KEY (CORRECT ANSWERS)

1. A
2. B
3. A
4. C
5. B

6. D
7. D
8. A
9. B
10. D

11. B
12. C
13. C
14. A
15. A

PREPARING WRITTEN MATERIAL

PARAGRAPH REARRANGEMENT
COMMENTARY

The sentences which follow are in scrambled order. You are to rearrange them in proper order and indicate the letter choice containing the correct answer at the space at the right.

Each group of sentences in this section is actually a paragraph presented in scrambled order. Each sentence in the group has a place in that paragraph; no sentence is to be left out. You are to read each group of sentences and decide upon the best order in which to put the sentences so as to form as well-organized paragraph.

The questions in this section measure the ability to solve a problem when all the facts relevant to its solution are not given.

More specifically, certain positions of responsibility and authority require the employee to discover connections between events sometimes, apparently, unrelated. In order to do this, the employee will find it necessary to correctly infer that unspecified events have probably occurred or are likely to occur. This ability becomes especially important when action must be taken on incomplete information.

Accordingly, these questions require competitors to choose among several suggested alternatives, each of which presents a different sequential arrangement of the events. Competitors must choose the MOST logical of the suggested sequences.

In order to do so, they may be required to draw on general knowledge to infer missing concepts or events that are essential to sequencing the given events. Competitors should be careful to infer only what is essential to the sequence. The plausibility of the wrong alternatives will always require the inclusion of unlikely events or of additional chains of events which are NOT essential to sequencing the given events.

It's very important to remember that you are looking for the best of the four possible choices, and that the best choice of all may not even be one of the answers you're given to choose from.

There is no one right way to solve these problems. Many people have found it helpful to first write out the order of the sentences, as they would have arranged them, on their scrap paper before looking at the possible answers. If their optimum answer is there, this can save them some time. If it isn't, this method can still give insight into solving the problem. Others find it most helpful to just go through each of the possible choices, contrasting each as they go along. You should use whatever method feels comfortable, and works, for you.

While most of these types of questions are not that difficult, we've added a higher percentage of the difficult type, just to give you more practice. Usually there are only one or two questions on this section that contain such subtle distinctions that you're unable to answer confidently, and you then may find yourself stuck deciding between two possible choices, neither of which you're sure about.

EXAMINATION SECTION
TEST 1

DIRECTIONS: The following groups of sentences need to be arranged in an order that makes sense. Select the letter preceding the sequence that represents the BEST sentence order. *PRINT THE LETTER OF THE CORRECT ANSWER IN THE SPACE AT THE RIGHT.*

1. I. The keyboard was purposely designed to be a little awkward to slow typists down.
    II. The arrangement of letters on the keyboard of a typewriter was not designed for the convenience of the typist.
    III. Fortunately, no one is suggesting that a new keyboard be designed right away.
    IV. If one were, we would have to learn to type all over again.
    V. The reason was that the early machines were slower than the typists and would jam easily.

    A. I, III, IV, II, V   B. II, V, I, IV, III
    C. V, I, II, III, IV   D. II, I, V, III, IV

    1.____

2. I. The majority of the new service jobs are part-time or low-paying.
    II. According to the U.S. Bureau of Labor Statistics, jobs in the service sector constitute 72% of all jobs in this country.
    III. If more and more workers receive less and less money, who will buy the goods and services needed to keep the economy going?
    IV. The service sector is by far the fastest growing part of the United States economy.
    V. Some economists look upon this trend with great concern.

    A. II, IV, I, V, III   B. II, III, IV, I, V
    C. V, IV, II, III, I   D. III, I, II, IV, V

    2.____

3. I. They can also affect one's endurance.
    II. This can stabilize blood sugar levels, and ensure that the brain is receiving a steady, constant supply of glucose, so that one is *hitting on all cylinders* while taking the test.
    III. By food, we mean real food, not junk food or unhealthy snacks.
    IV. For this reason, it is important not to skip a meal, and to bring food with you to the exam.
    V. One's blood sugar levels can affect how clearly one is able to think and concentrate during an exam.

    A. V, IV, II, III, I   B. V, II, I, IV, III
    C. V, I, IV, III, II   D. V, IV, I, III, II

    3.____

4. I. Those who are the embodiment of desire are absorbed in material quests, and those who are the embodiment of feeling are warriors who value power more than possession.
    II. These qualities are in everyone, but in different degrees.
    III. But those who value understanding yearn not for goods or victory, but for knowledge.
    IV. According to Plato, human behavior flows from three main sources: desire, emotion, and knowledge,

    4.____

75

V. In the perfect state, the industrial forces would produce but not rule, the military would protect but not rule, and the forces of knowledge, the philosopher kings, would reign.

A. IV, V, I, II, III
B. V, I, II, III, IV
C. IV, III, II, I, V
D. IV, II, I, III, V

5.
I. Of the more than 26,000 tons of garbage produced daily in New York City, 12,000 tons arrive daily at Fresh Kills.
II. In a month, enough garbage accumulates there to fill the Empire State Building.
III. In 1937, the Supreme Court halted the practice of dumping the trash of New York City into the sea.
IV. Although the garbage is compacted, in a few years the mounds of garbage at Fresh Kills will be the highest points south of Maine's Mount Desert Island on the Eastern Seaboard.
V. Instead, tugboats now pull barges of much of the trash to Staten Island and the largest landfill in the world, Fresh Kills.

A. III, V, IV, I, II
B. III, V, II, IV, I
C. III, V, I, II, IV
D. III, II, V, IV, I

6.
I. Communists rank equality very high, but freedom very low.
II. Unlike communists, conservatives place a high value on freedom and a very low value on equality.
III. A recent study demonstrated that one way to classify people's political beliefs is to look at the importance placed on two words: freedom and equality.
IV. Thus, by demonstrating how members of these groups feel about the two words, the study has proved to be useful for political analysts in several European countries.
V. According to the study, socialists and liberals rank both freedom and equality very high, while fascists rate both very low.

A. III, V, I, II, IV
B. III, IV, V, I, II
C. III, V, IV, II, I
D. III, I, II, IV, V

7.
I. "Can there be anything more amazing than this?"
II. If the riddle is successfully answered, his dead brothers will be brought back to life.
III. "Even though man sees those around him dying every day," says Dharmaraj, "he still believes and acts as if he were immortal."
IV. "What is the cause of ceaseless wonder?" asks the Lord of the Lake.
V. In the ancient epic, The Mahabharata, a riddle is asked of one of the Pandava brothers.

A. V, II, I, IV, III
B. V, IV, III, I, II
C. V, II, IV, III, I
D. V, II, IV, I, III

8.
   I. On the contrary, the two main theories — the cooperative (neoclassical) theory and the radical (labor theory) — clearly rest on very different assumptions, which have very different ethical overtones.
   II. The distribution of income is the primary factor in determining the relative levels of material well-being that different groups or individuals attain.
   III. Of all issues in economics, the distribution of income is one of the most controversial.
   IV. The neoclassical theory tends to support the existing income distribution (or minor changes), while the labor theory tends to support substantial changes in the way income is distributed.
   V. The intensity of the controversy reflects the fact that different economic theories are not purely neutral, *detached* theories with no ethical or moral implications.

   A. II, I, V, IV, III
   B. III, II, V, I, IV
   C. III, V, II, I, IV
   D. III, V, IV, I, II

   8.____

9.
   I. The pool acts as a broker and ensures that the cheapest power gets used first.
   II. Every six seconds, the pool's computer monitors all of the generating stations in the state and decides which to ask for more power and which to cut back.
   III. The buying and selling of electrical power is handled by the New York Power Pool in Guilderland, New York.
   IV. This is to the advantage of both the buying and selling utilities.
   V. The pool began operation in 1970, and consists of the state's eight electric utilities.

   A. V, I, II, III, IV
   B. IV, II, I, III, V
   C. III, V, I, IV, II
   D. V, III, IV, II, I

   9.____

10.
    I. Modern English is much simpler grammatically than Old English.
    II. Finnish grammar is very complicated; there are some fifteen cases, for example.
    III. Chinese, a very old language, may seem to be the exception, but it is the great number of characters/ words that must be mastered that makes it so difficult to learn, not its grammar.
    IV. The newest literary language — that is, written as well as spoken — is Finnish, whose literary roots go back only to about the middle of the nineteenth century.
    V. Contrary to popular belief, the longer a language is been in use the simpler its grammar — not the reverse.

    A. IV, I, II, III, V
    B. V, I, IV, II, III
    C. I, II, IV, III, V
    D. IV, II, III, I, V

    10.____

KEY (CORRECT ANSWERS)

1. D
2. A
3. C
4. D
5. C

6. A
7. C
8. B
9. C
10. B

TEST 2

DIRECTIONS: This type of question tests your ability to recognize accurate paraphrasing, well-constructed paragraphs, and appropriate style and tone. It is important that the answer you select contains only the facts or concepts given in the original sentences. It is also important that you be aware of incomplete sentences, inappropriate transitions, unsupported opinions, incorrect usage, and illogical sentence order. Paragraphs that do not include all the necessary facts and concepts, that distort them, or that add new ones are not considered correct.

The format for this section may vary. Sometimes, long paragraphs are given, and emphasis is placed on style and organization. Our first five questions are of this type. Other times, the paragraphs are shorter, and there is less emphasis on style and more emphasis on accurate representation of information. Our second group of five questions are of this nature.

For each of Questions 1 through 10, select the paragraph that BEST expresses the ideas contained in the sentences above it. *PRINT THE LETTER OF THE CORRECT ANSWER IN THE SPACE AT THE RIGHT.*

1. I. Listening skills are very important for managers.
    II. Listening skills are not usually emphasized.
    III. Whenever managers are depicted in books, manuals or the media, they are always talking, never listening.
    IV. We'd like you to read the enclosed handout on listening skills and to try to consciously apply them this week.
    V. We guarantee they will improve the quality of your interactions.

    A. Unfortunately, listening skills are not usually emphasized for managers. Managers are always depicted as talking, never listening. We'd like you to read the enclosed handout on listening skills. Please try to apply these principles this week. If you do, we guarantee they will improve the quality of your interactions.
    B. The enclosed handout on listening skills will be important improving the quality of your interactions. We guarantee it. All you have to do is take some time this week to read it and to consciously try to apply the principles. Listening skills are very important for managers, but they are not usually emphasized. Whenever managers are depicted in books, manuals or the media, they are always talking, never listening.
    C. Listening well is one of the most important skills a manager can have, yet it's not usually given much attention. Think about any representation of managers in books, manuals, or in the media that you may have seen. They're always talking, never listening. We'd like you to read the enclosed handout on listening skills and consciously try to apply them the rest of the week. We guarantee you will see a difference in the quality of your interactions.
    D. Effective listening, one very important tool in the effective manager's arsenal, is usually not emphasized enough. The usual depiction of managers in books, manuals or the media is one in which they are always talking, never listening. We'd like you to read the enclosed handout and consciously try to apply the information contained therein throughout the rest of the week. We feel sure that you will see a marked difference in the quality of your interactions.

1.____

2.
I. Chekhov wrote three dramatic masterpieces which share certain themes and formats: Uncle Vanya, The Cherry Orchard, and The Three Sisters.
II. They are primarily concerned with the passage of time and how this erodes human aspirations.
III. The plays are haunted by the ghosts of the wasted life.
IV. The characters are concerned with life's lesser problems; however, such as the inability to make decisions, loyalty to the wrong cause, and the inability to be clear.
V. This results in a sweet, almost aching, type of a sadness referred to as Chekhovian.

2.____

A. Chekhov wrote three dramatic masterpieces: Uncle Vanya, The Cherry Orchard, and The Three Sisters. These masterpieces share certain themes and formats: the passage of time, how time erodes human aspirations, and the ghosts of wasted life. Each masterpiece is characterized by a sweet, almost aching, type of sadness that has become known as Chekhovian. The sweetness of this sadness hinges on the fact that it is not the great tragedies of life which are destroying these characters, but their minor flaws: indecisiveness, misplaced loyalty, unclarity.

B. The Cherry Orchard, Uncle Vanya, and The Three Sisters are three dramatic masterpieces written by Chekhov that use similar formats to explore a common theme. Each is primarily concerned with the way that passing time wears down human aspirations, and each is haunted by the ghosts of the wasted life. The characters are shown struggling futilely with the lesser problems of life: indecisiveness, loyalty to the wrong cause, and the inability to be clear. These struggles create a mood of sweet, almost aching, sadness that has become known as Chekhovian.

C. Chekhov's dramatic masterpieces are, along with The Cherry Orchard, Uncle Vanya, and The Three Sisters. These plays share certain thematic and formal similarities. They are concerned most of all with the passage of time and the way in which time erodes human aspirations. Each play is haunted by the specter of the wasted life. Chekhov's characters are caught, however, by life's lesser snares: indecisiveness, loyalty to the wrong cause, and unclarity. The characteristic mood is a sweet, almost aching type of sadness that has come to be known as Chekhovian.

D. A Chekhovian mood is characterized by sweet, almost aching, sadness. The term comes from three dramatic tragedies by Chekhov which revolve around the sadness of a wasted life. The three masterpieces (Uncle Vanya, The Three Sisters, and The Cherry Orchard) share the same theme and format. The plays are concerned with how the passage of time erodes human aspirations. They are peopled with characters who are struggling with life's lesser problems. These are people who are indecisive, loyal to the wrong causes, or are unable to make themselves clear.

3.   I. Movie previews have often helped producers decide what parts of movies they should take out or leave in.   3.____
        II. The first 1933 preview of King Kong was very helpful to the producers because many people ran screaming from the theater and would not return when four men first attacked by Kong were eaten by giant spiders.
       III. The 1950 premiere of Sunset Boulevard resulted in the filming of an entirely new beginning, and a delay of six months in the film's release.
      IV. In the original opening scene, William Holden was in a morgue talking with thirty-six other "corpses" about the ways some of them had died.
       V. When he began to tell them of his life with Gloria Swanson, the audience found this hilarious, instead of taking the scene seriously.

      A. Movie previews have often helped producers decide what parts of movies they should leave in or take out. For example, the first preview of King Kong in 1933 was very helpful. In one scene, four men were first attacked by Kong and then eaten by giant spiders. Many members of the audience ran screaming from the theater and would not return. The premiere of the 1950 film Sunset Boulevard was also very helpful. In the original opening scene, William Holden was in a morgue with thirty-six other "corpses," discussing the ways some of them had died. When he began to tell them of his life with Gloria Swanson, the audience found this hilarious. They were supposed to take the scene seriously. The result was a delay of six months in the release of the film while a new beginning was added.

      B. Movie previews have often helped producers decide whether they should change various parts of a movie. After the 1933 preview of King Kong, a scene in which four men who had been attacked by Kong were eaten by giant spiders was taken out as many people ran screaming from the theater and would not return. The 1950 premiere of Sunset Boulevard also led to some changes. In the original opening scene, William Holden was in a morgue talking with thirty-six other "corpses" about the ways some of them had died. When he began to tell them of his life with Gloria Swanson, the audience found this hilarious, instead of taking the scene seriously.

      C. What do Sunset Boulevard and King Kong have in common? Both show the value of using movie previews to test audience reaction. The first 1933 preview of King Kong showed that a scene showing four men being eaten by giant spiders after having been attacked by Kong was too frightening for many people. They ran screaming from the theater and couldn't be coaxed back. The 1950 premiere of Sunset Boulevard was also a scream, but not the kind the producers intended. The movie opens with William Holden lying in a morgue discussing the ways they had died with thirty-six other "corpses." When he began to tell them of his life with Gloria Swanson, the audience couldn't take him seriously. Their laughter caused a six-month delay while the beginning was rewritten.

      D. Producers very often use movie previews to decide if changes are needed. The premiere of Sunset Boulevard in 1950 led to a new beginning and a six-month delay in film release. At the beginning, William Holden and thirty-six other "corpses" discuss the ways some of them died. Rather than taking this seriously, the audience thought it was hilarious when he began to tell them of his life with Gloria Swanson. The first 1933 preview of King Kong was very helpful for its producers because one scene so terrified the audience that many of them ran screaming from the theater and would not return. In this particular scene, four men who had first been attacked by Kong were being eaten by giant spiders.

4.
I. It is common for supervisors to view employees as "things" to be manipulated.
II. This approach does not motivate employees, nor does the carrot-and-stick approach because employees often recognize these behaviors and resent them.
III. Supervisors can change these behaviors by using self-inquiry and persistence.
IV. The best managers genuinely respect those they work with, are supportive and helpful, and are interested in working as a team with those they supervise.
V. They disagree with the Golden Rule that says "he or she who has the gold makes the rules."

4.____

A. Some managers act as if they think the Golden Rule means "he or she who has the gold makes the rules." They show disrespect to employees by seeing them as "things" to be manipulated. Obviously, this approach does not motivate employees any more than the carrot-and-stick approach motivates them. The employees are smart enough to spot these behaviors and resent them. On the other hand, the managers genuinely respect those they work with, are supportive and helpful, and are interested in working as a team. Self-inquiry and persistence can change even the former type of supervisor into the latter.

B. Many supervisors fall into the trap of viewing employees as "things" to be manipulated, or try to motivate them by using a earrot-and-stick approach. These methods do not motivate employees, who often recognize the behaviors and resent them. Supervisors can change these behaviors, however, by using self-inquiry and persistence. The best managers are supportive and helpful, and have genuine respect for those with whom they work. They are interested in working as a team with those they supervise. To them, the Golden Rule is not "he or she who has the gold makes the rules."

C. Some supervisors see employees as "things" to be used or manipulated using a carrot-and-stick technique. These methods don't work. Employees often see through them and resent them. A supervisor who wants to change may do so. The techniques of self-inquiry and persistence can be used to turn him or her into the type of supervisor who doesn't think the Golden Rule is "he or she who has the gold makes the rules." They may become like the best managers who treat those with whom they work with respect and give them help and support. These are the managers who know how to build a team.

D. Unfortunately, many supervisors act as if their employees are objects whose movements they can position at will. This mistaken belief has the same result as another popular motivational technique—the carrot-and-stick approach. Both attitudes can lead to the same result — resentment from those employees who recognize the behaviors for what they are. Supervisors who recognize these behaviors can change through the use of persistence and the use of self-inquiry. It's important to remember that the best managers respect their employees. They readily give necessary help and support and are interested in working as a team with those they supervise. To these managers, the Golden Rule is not "he or she who has the gold makes the rules."

5. I.   The first half of the nineteenth century produced a group of pessimistic poets — Byron, De Musset, Heine, Pushkin, and Leopardi.
    II. It also produced a group of pessimistic composers—Schubert, Chopin, Schumann, and even the later Beethoven.
    III. Above all, in philosophy, there was the profoundly pessimistic philosopher, Schopenhauer.
    IV. The Revolution was dead, the Bourbons were restored, the feudal barons were reclaiming their land, and progress everywhere was being suppressed, as the great age was over.
    V.   "I thank God," said Goethe, "that I am not young in so thoroughly finished a world."

5._____

A. "I thank God," said Goethe, "that I am not young in so thoroughly finished a world." The Revolution was dead, the Bourbons were restored, the feudal barons were reclaiming their land, and progress everywhere was being suppressed. The first half of the nineteenth century produced a group of pessimistic poets: Byron, De Musset, Heine, Pushkin, and Leopardi. It also produced pessimistic composers: Schubert, Chopin, Schumann. Although Beethoven came later, he fits into this group, too. Finally and above all, it also produced a profoundly pessimistic philosopher, Schopenhauer. The great age was over.
B. The first half of the nineteenth century produced a group of pessimistic poets: Byron, De Musset, Heine, Pushkin, and Leopardi. It produced a group of pessimistic composers: Schubert, Chopin, Schumann, and even the later Beethoven. Above all, it produced a profoundly pessimistic philosopher, Schopenhauer. For each of these men, the great age was over. The Revolution was dead, and the Bourbons were restored. The feudal barons were reclaiming their land, and progress everywhere was being suppressed.
C. The great age was over. The Revolution was dead—the Bourbons were restored, and the feudal barons were reclaiming their land. Progress everywhere was being suppressed. Out of this climate came a profound pessimism. Poets, like Byron, De Musset, Heine, Pushkin, and Leopardi; composers, like Schubert, Chopin, Schumann, and even the later Beethoven; and, above all, a profoundly pessimistic philosopher, Schopenauer. This pessimism which arose in the first half of the nineteenth century is illustrated by these words of Goethe, "I thank God that I am not young in so thoroughly finished a world."
D. The first half of the nineteenth century produced a group of pessimistic poets, Byron, De Musset, Heine, Pushkin, and Leopardi — and a group of pessimistic composers, Schubert, Chopin, Schumann, and the later Beethoven. Above all, it produced a profoundly pessimistic philosopher, Schopenhauer. The great age was over. The Revolution was dead, the Bourbons were restored, the feudal barons were reclaiming their land, and progress everywhere was being suppressed. "I thank God," said Goethe, "that I am not young in so thoroughly finished a world."

6. I.   A new manager sometimes may feel insecure about his or her competence in the new position.
    II. The new manager may then exhibit defensive or arrogant behavior towards those one supervises, or the new manager may direct overly flattering behavior toward one's new supervisor.

6._____

A. Sometimes, a new manager may feel insecure about his or her ability to perform well in this new position. The insecurity may lead him or her to treat others differently. He or she may display arrogant or defensive behavior towards those he or she supervises, or be overly flattering to his or her new supervisor.
B. A new manager may sometimes feel insecure about his or her ability to perform well in the new position. He or she may then become arrogant, defensive, or overly flattering towards those he or she works with.
C. There are times when a new manager may be insecure about how well he or she can perform in the new job. The new manager may also behave defensive or act in an arrogant way towards those he or she supervises, or overly flatter his or her boss.
D. Sometimes, a new manager may feel insecure about his or her ability to perform well in the new position. He or she may then display arrogant or defensive behavior towards those they supervise, or become overly flattering towards their supervisors.

7.
I. It is possible to eliminate unwanted behavior by bringing it under stimulus control — tying the behavior to a cue, and then never, or rarely, giving the cue.
II. One trainer successfully used this method to keep an energetic young porpoise from coming out of her tank whenever she felt like it, which was potentially dangerous.
III. Her trainer taught her to do it for a reward, in response to a hand signal, and then rarely gave the signal.

7.____

A. Unwanted behavior can be eliminated by tying the behavior to a cue, and then never, or rarely, giving the cue. This is called stimulus control. One trainer was able to use this method to keep an energetic young porpoise from coming out of her tank by teaching her to come out for a reward in response to a hand signal, and then rarely giving the signal.
B. Stimulus control can be used to eliminate unwanted behavior. In this method, behavior is tied to a cue, and then the cue is rarely, if ever, given. One trainer was able to successfully use stimulus control to keep an energetic young porpoise from coming out of her tank whenever she felt like it — a potentially dangerous practice. She taught the porpoise to come out for a reward when she gave a hand signal, and then rarely gave the signal.
C. It is possible to eliminate behavior that is undesirable by bringing it under stimulus control by tying behavior to a signal, and then rarely giving the signal. One trainer successfully used this method to keep an energetic young porpoise from coming out of her tank, a potentially dangerous situation. Her trainer taught the porpoise to do it for a reward, in response to a hand signal, and then would rarely give the signal.
D. By using stimulus control, it is possible to eliminate unwanted behavior by tying the behavior to a cue, and then rarely or never give the cue. One trainer was able to use this method to successfully stop a young porpoise from coming out of her tank whenever she felt like it. To curb this potentially dangerous practice, the porpoise was taught by the trainer to come out of the tank for a reward, in response to a hand signal, and then rarely given the signal.

8. I. There is a great deal of concern over the safety of commercial trucks, caused by their greatly increased role in serious accidents since federal deregulation in 1981.
   II. Recently, 60 percent of trucks in New York and Connecticut and 70 percent of trucks in Maryland randomly stopped by state troopers failed safety inspections.
   III. Sixteen states in the United States require no training at all for truck drivers.

   A. Since federal deregulation in 1981, there has been a great deal of concern over the safety of commercial trucks, and their greatly increased role in serious accidents. Recently, 60 percent of trucks in New York and Connecticut, and 70 percent of trucks in Maryland failed safety inspections. Sixteen states in the United States require no training at all for truck drivers.
   B. There is a great deal of concern over the safety of commercial trucks since federal deregulation in 1981. Their role in serious accidents has greatly increased. Recently, 60 percent of trucks randomly stopped in Connecticut and New York, and 70 percent in Maryland failed safety inspections conducted by state troopers. Sixteen states in the United States provide no training at all for truck drivers.
   C. Commercial trucks have a greatly increased role in serious accidents since federal deregulation in 1981. This has led to a great deal of concern. Recently, 70 percent of trucks in Maryland and 60 percent of trucks in New York and Connecticut failed inspection of those that were randomly stopped by state troopers. Sixteen states in the United States require no training for all truck drivers.
   D. Since federal deregulation in 1981, the role that commercial trucks have played in serious accidents has greatly increased, and this has led to a great deal of concern. Recently, 60 percent of trucks in New York and Connecticut, and 70 percent of trucks in Maryland randomly stopped by state troopers failed safety inspections. Sixteen states in the U.S. don't require any training for truck drivers.

8.____

9. I. No matter how much some people have, they still feel unsatisfied and want more, or want to keep what they have forever.
   II. One recent television documentary showed several people flying from New York to Paris for a one-day shopping spree to buy platinum earrings, because they were bored.
   III. In Brazil, some people are ordering coffins that cost a minimum of $45,000 and are equipping them with deluxe stereos, televisions and other graveyard necessities.

   A. Some people, despite having a great deal, still feel unsatisfied and want more, or think they can keep what they have forever. One recent documentary on television showed several people enroute from Paris to New York for a one day shopping spree to buy platinum earrings, because they were bored. Some people in Brazil are even ordering coffins equipped with such graveyard necessities as deluxe stereos and televisions. The price of the coffins start at $45,000.
   B. No matter how much some people have, they may feel unsatisfied. This leads them to want more, or to want to keep what they have forever. Recently, a television documentary depicting several people flying from New York to Paris for a one day shopping spree to buy platinum earrings. They were bored. Some people in Brazil are ordering coffins that cost at least $45,000 and come equipped with deluxe televisions, stereos and other necessary graveyard items.
   C. Some people will be dissatisfied no matter how much they have. They may want more, or they may want to keep what they have forever. One recent television documentary showed several people, motivated by boredom, jetting from New York to

9.____

8 (#2)

Paris for a one-day shopping spree to buy platinum earrings. In Brazil, some people are ordering coffins equipped with deluxe stereos, televisions and other graveyard necessities. The minimum price for these coffins - $45,000.

D. Some people are never satisfied. No matter how much they have they still want more, or think they can keep what they have forever. One television documentary recently showed several people flying from New York to Paris for the day to buy platinum earrings because they were bored. In Brazil, some people are ordering coffins that cost $45,000 and are equipped with deluxe stereos, televisions and other graveyard necessities.

10.
   I. A television signal or Video signal has three parts.
   II. Its parts are the black-and-white portion, the color portion, and the synchronizing (sync) pulses, which keep the picture stable.
   III. Each video source, whether it's a camera or a video-cassette recorder, contains its own generator of these synchronizing pulses to accompany the picture that it's sending in order to keep it steady and straight.
   IV. In order to produce a clean recording, a video-cassette recorder must "lock-up" to the sync pulses that are part of the video it is trying to record, and this effort may be very noticeable if the device does not have genlock.

10.____

A. There are three parts to a television or video signal: the black-and-white part, the color part, and the synchronizing (sync) pulses, which keep the picture stable. Whether it's a video-cassette recorder or a camera, each each video source contains its own pulse that synchronizes and generates the picture it's sending in order to keep it straight and steady. A video-cassette recorder must "lock up" to the sync pulses that are part of the video it's trying to record. If the device doesn't have genlock, this effort must be very noticeable.

B. A video signal or television is comprised of three parts: the black-and-white portion, the color portion, and the the sync (synchronizing) pulses, which keep the picture stable. Whether it's a camera or a video-cassette recorder, each video source contains its own generator of these synchronizing pulses. These accompany the picture that it's sending in order to keep it straight and steady. A video-cassette recorder must "lock up" to the sync pulses that are part of the video it is trying to record in order to produce a clean recording. This effort may be very noticeable if the device does not have genlock.

C. There are three parts to a television or video signal: the color portion, the black-and-white portion, and the sync (synchronizing pulses). These keep the picture stable. Each video source, whether it's a video-cassette recorder or a camera, generates these synchronizing pulses accompanying the picture it's sending in order to keep it straight and steady. If a clean recording is to be produced, a video-cassette recorder must store the sync pulses that are part of the video it is trying to record. This effort may not be noticeable if the device does not have genlock.

D. A television signal or video signal has three parts: the black-and-white portion, the color portion, and the synchronizing (sync) pulses. It's the sync pulses which keep the picture stable, which accompany it and keep it steady and straight. Whether it's a camera or a video-cassette recorder, each video source contains its own generator of these synchronizing pulses. To produce a clean recording, a video-cassette recorder must "lock-up" to the sync pulses that are part of the video it is trying to record. If the device does not have genlock, this effort may be very noticeable.

KEY (CORRECT ANSWERS)

1. C
2. B
3. A
4. B
5. D

6. A
7. B
8. D
9. C
10. D

EXAMINATION SECTION
TEST 1

DIRECTIONS: Each question or incomplete statement is followed by several suggested answers or completions. Select the one that BEST answers the question or completes the statement. *PRINT THE LETTER OF THE CORRECT ANSWER IN THE SPACE AT THE RIGHT.*

Questions 1-4.

DIRECTIONS: Questions 1 through 4 are to be answered on the basis of the following passage.

A State department which is interested in finding acceptable solutions to the operational problems of specific types of community self-help organizations recently sent two of its staff members to meet with one such organization. At that meeting, the leaders of the community organization voiced the need for increased activity planning input of a more detailed nature from the citizens regularly served by that organization. There followed a discussion of a number of information-gathering methods, including surveys by telephone, questionnaires mailed to the citizens' residences, in-person interviews with the citizens, and the placing of suggestion boxes in the organization's headquarters building. Concern was expressed by one of the leaders that the organization's funds be spent judiciously. The State department representatives present promised to investigate the possibility of a matching fund grant of money to the organization.

Later, the proposed survey was conducted using questionnaires completed by those citizens who visited the organization's headquarters. The results of the survey included the information that twice as many citizens wanted more educational activities scheduled than wanted more social activities scheduled, whereas one-half of those who wanted more educational activities scheduled were interested mainly in special job training.

1. A similar survey conducted by a State department employee involved special job training. That survey uncovered the information below. The following four sentences are to be rearranged to form the most effective and logical paragraph. Select the letter representing the best sequence for these sentences.
   I. The majority of those who are still in this group are ethnic minorities.
   II. The number of economically disadvantaged people who enjoyed their special job training is larger than the number of economically disadvantaged people who did not enjoy it.
   III. Thirty-five percent of all those who are economically disadvantaged are not ethnic minorities.
   IV. Eighty percent of those who have completed special job training in the past ten years are economically disadvantaged.
   The CORRECT answer is:

   A. IV, I, III, II   B. I, III, II, IV
   C. IV, II, I, III   D. I, II, III, IV

2. In the reading passage above, the word *judiciously* means MOST NEARLY

   A. legally   B. immediately
   C. prudently   D. uniformly

1.____

2.____

3. Based *only* on the information in the reading passage, which one of the following statements is MOST fully supported?　　3.____

   A. The leaders of the community organization in question wanted to increase the quantity and quality of feedback about that organization's suggestion boxes.
   B. The number of citizens surveyed who wanted more educational activities scheduled and were mainly interested in special job training was the same as the number of citizens surveyed who wanted more social activities to be scheduled.
   C. At the meeting concerned, matching funds were promised to the community organization in question by the two State department representatives present.
   D. Telephone surveys generally yield more accurate information than do surveys conducted through the use of mailed questionnaires.

4. The following four sentences are to be rearranged to form the most effective and logical paragraph. Select the letter representing the best sequence for these sentences.　　4.____
      I. Formal surveys of citizens within a community also convey to those citizens the interest of the community leadership in hearing the citizens' ideas about community improvement.
      II. Such surveys can provide needed input into the process of establishing specific community program goals.
      III. Formally conducted surveys of community residents often yield valuable information to the local area leaders responsible for community-based programs.
      IV. No community should formulate these goals without attempting to obtain the views of its citizenry.
   The CORRECT answer is:

   A. III, I, IV, II　　　　　　　　　　B. I, III, II, IV
   C. III, II, IV, I　　　　　　　　　　D. IV, III, II, I

Questions 5-8.

DIRECTIONS: Questions 5 through 8 are to be answered on the basis of the following passage.

The Smith Paint Company, which currently employs 2,000 persons, has been in existence for 20 years. A new chemical paint, Futuron, was recently developed by an employee of that company. This paint was released for public use a month ago on a trial basis. The sales were phenomenal, and there is a great demand for more Futuron to be manufactured. The profits to be made by increased manufacturing and sale of Futuron could place the Smith Paint Company in a leading role in the paint industry.

The Smith Paint Company currently produces 2 million gallons of the more traditional paint per year. The Smith Paint Company's Board of Directors wishes to reduce its production of this traditional paint by 50%, and to produce 1 million gallons of Futuron per year.

The employees are quite concerned about this potential production change. A public nonprofit research group has been investigating the chemical make-up of Futuron. Initial research indicates that negative physical reactions may result from working closely with the chemicals necessary to manufacture Futuron. For this reason, most of the company employees do not want the proposed change in production to occur. The members of the Board of Directors, however, argue that the research results are too inconclusive to cause great concern. They say that the company would lose 25% to 50% of its potential profit if the large-scale manufacturing of Futuron is not initiated immediately.

5. Seventy-five percent of the Smith Paint Company's current employees were hired during its first 10 years of operation. Fifteen percent were hired in the past five years. During the five-year interval between the first ten years and the most recent five years, 40 persons were hired per year.
   What percentage of its total employees were hired during the Smith Paint Company's first 13 years of operation?

   A. 75%   B. 81%   C. 85%   D. 90%

6. Assume that the total possible profit the Smith Paint Company could make during its first year of manufacturing the proposed amount of Futuron would be $1.00 per gallon. The purchase of new machinery would reduce this first-year profit by 50%. The anticipated delay, during the first production year, in establishing large-scale manufacturing facilities would reduce the total possible profit by an additional 25%.
   Given this information, what would be the actual profit made from the first year of manufacturing Futuron?

   A. $250,000   B. $375,000   C. $500,000   D. $750,000

7. In the reading passage, the word *inconclusive* means MOST NEARLY

   A. ineluctable   B. incorrect
   C. unreasonable   D. indeterminate

8. Based on the information in the reading passage, which of the following statements represents the MOST accurate conclusion?

   A. The proposed reduction in the production of its traditional paint would not financially injure the Smith Paint Company.
   B. A greater proportion of the Smith Paint Company's employees are in favor of the proposed increase in Futuron production than are opposed to it.
   C. The increased Futuron production proposed by the Smith Paint Company's Board of Directors would cause that company's employees considerable health damage.
   D. Positive public response to the sale of Futuron suggests that considerable profit can be made by increasing the manufacturing and sale of Futuron.

KEY (CORRECT ANSWERS)

1. A
2. C
3. B
4. C
5. B
6. A
7. D
8. D

SOLUTIONS TO PROBLEMS

1. For the following reasons, Choice A is correct and the other three choices are incorrect:

    1. Both Choice B and Choice D begin with Sentence I, which states, *The majority of those who are still in this group are ethnic minorities.* The paragraph cannot logically begin with a statement such as Sentence I, because no one reading the paragraph would know what *this group* refers to. Therefore, Choice B and Choice D are not correct and may be eliminated from consideration.

    2. Both Choice A and Choice C begin with Sentence IV, which states, *Eighty percent of those who have completed special job training in the past ten years are economically disadvantaged.* The problem then becomes selecting the best sequence of the other three sentences so that they most logically follow the initial Sentence IV.

    3. If you select Choice C, then you are choosing Sentence II as the correct second sentence. Sentence II states, *The number of economically disadvantaged people who enjoyed their special job training is larger than the number of economically disadvantaged people who did not enjoy it.* Then Sentence I would be the third sentence. However, that would not be logical, because you could not tell whether *this group* in Sentence I refers to *economically disadvantaged people who enjoyed their special job training* or whether *this group* refers to *economically disadvantaged people who did not enjoy it.* Therefore, Choice C is not correct.

    4. By the process of elimination, only Choice A remains. Choice A specifies Sentence I as the second sentence, which is logically correct in that *this group* in Sentence I will then refer to those who *are economically disadvantaged* in Sentence IV. The two remaining sentences also refer back to *economically disadvantaged,* thus creating a paragraph that reads logically from start to finish. Therefore, Choice A is the correct answer.

2. Choices B and D should be eliminated from further consideration due to the context in which the word *judiciously* was used in the reading passage. Specifically, concern was expressed that funds be spent judiciously. Nothing in the paragraph suggests a need for concern if the funds were not spent immediately or uniformly. Choice A must be considered, because public funds should be spent legally. However, the word *judiciously* is related to the word *judgment* rather than to the word *judiciary.* It is the latter word that has to do with courts of law and is related to legality, so Choice A is incorrect. On the other hand, *judiciously* and *prudently* both mean *wisely* and *with direction*. Therefore, Choice C is correct.

3. Choice B is the correct choice. No matter what numbers you apply, Choice B still will be correct. This is because when you multiply any number by two and then divide the result in half, you end up with the same number that you began with. For example, suppose that 20 citizens wanted more social activities. Twice that number (40 citizens) wanted more educational activities. But of those 40 citizens, one-half (20 citizens) wanted mainly special job training.

Choice A is incorrect because, first of all, the organization did not have any suggestion boxes; although suggestion boxes were discussed, questionnaires ultimately were used instead. In addition, Choice A is incorrect because it was input about the planning of activities that the leaders of the community organization wanted rather than feedback concerning suggestion boxes.

Choice C also is not correct. Instead of promising the matching funds, the State department representatives promised to investigate (or look into) the possibility of obtaining the matching funds.

Choice D is incorrect because the reading passage does not tell whether telephone surveys or mailed questionnaires provide more accurate information. Remember, the instructions for this question state that the question is to be answered based ONLY on the information in the applicable reading passage.

4. The correct answer is Choice C. Choice A and Choice C both begin with Sentence III, which certainly could be the logical first sentence of a paragraph. However, the next sentence (Sentence I) in Choice A leaves the initial topic of obtaining information from citizens. The third sentence in Choice A would be Sentence IV, *No community should formulate these goals without attempting to obtain the views of its citizenry.* The words *these goals* do not logically refer to anything in the previous two sentences, so Choice A is incorrect.

Choice B also is incorrect because the word *also* in its first sentence (Sentence I) has nothing to logically refer to. *Also* would have to be used in a sentence that comes later in the paragraph.

Choice D has the same problem as Choice A. Choice D begins with Sentence IV, which starts off, *No community should formulate these goals....* Again, the words *these goals* need to refer to something in a previous sentence about goals in order to be logically correct.

5. Choice B is correct. Here are the mathematical computations you might use to arrive at the correct answer of 81%:

   1. The reading passage states that the Smith Paint Company currently employs 2,000 persons. The first part of this question states that 75% of those current employees were hired during the first ten years that the company was in operation. By multiplying 75% by 2,000, you would find that 1,500 of the current employees were hired during the company's first ten years.

   2. The question asks about the first 13 years of the company's operation rather than just the first ten years. Therefore, you need the arithmetical information for the three years that immediately followed the first ten years. You know from the reading passage that the company has been operating for 20 years. You have the information for the first ten years. Twenty minus ten leaves the most recent ten years.

3. You know from the question that 40 persons were hired each year during the five-year period of time between the first ten years and the most recent five years. However, you need information about only the first three years. By multiplying 40 persons per year by three years, you would find that 120 people were hired during the first three years that came immediately after the first ten years of the company's operation.

4. Next, you would need to add 1,500 people (for the first ten years) and 120 people (for the next three years). That would give you a total of 1,620 people hired during the first 13 years.

5. The question asks for the percentage of the Smith Paint Company's total employees hired during its first 13 years. You know that the total number of employees is 2,000. The question then is: 1,620 people is what percentage of 2,000 people? By dividing 2,000 into 1,620, you would find that the correct answer is 81%.

Choice A is incorrect because it deals with only the first ten years that the company was in operation, rather than the first 13 years. If you took 1,500 people (from Step 1 in the explanatory material for the correct answer) and divided that number by 2,000 people, you would arrive at 75%, which is not correct.

Choice C is incorrect. If you correctly arrived at 1,500 people for the first ten years but then incorrectly dealt with the next five years instead of the next three years, you would end up with the wrong answer of 85%. First, you would multiply 40 people by five years and end up with 200 people. Next, you would add 200 to 1,500 and end up with 1,700 people. Finally, you would divide 1,700 by 2,000 and get 85%.

Choice D also is incorrect. If you correctly arrived at 1,500 people for the first ten years but then used the information for the most recent five years instead of the information for the five years that came just before the most recent five years, you would end up with the incorrect answer of 90%. First, you would find from the question that 15% of the total employees were hired in the past five years. Next, you would multiply 15% by 2,000 total employees and end up with 300. Next, you would add 1,500 employees and 300 employees, ending up with a total of 1,800 employees. By dividing 1,800 by 2,000, you would arrive at 90%.

6. Choice A is correct. Here are the mathematical computations you would need to make to arrive at the correct answer of $250,000:

   1. The reading passage states that the amount of Futuron proposed for manufacture each year is 1 million gallons. The question states that the possible profit per gallon would be $1.00. By multiplying $1.00 by 1,000,000, you would find that $1,000,000 would be the total possible profit to be made during the first year.

   2. The question states that the $1,000,000 possible profit would have to be reduced by 50% because of the purchase of new machinery, plus by an additional 25% due to the delay in establishing manufacturing facilities. The possible profit must, therefore, be reduced by 50% plus 25%, or by a total of 75%, leaving only 25% of the $1,000,000 as possible profit.

3. By multiplying 25% by $1,000,000, you would arrive at $250,000 as the actual profit which would be made.

Choice B is incorrect. If the two profit reductions were incorrectly multiplied by one another (50% times 25%) and the product (12 1/2%) added to 50%, there would have been a net reduction of 62 1/2%, yielding $375,000. However, the two profit reductions are independent of each other and should be added together.

Choice C also is incorrect. It would occur if you only took into account the 50% profit reduction. However, as the paragraph states, you must also deduct an additional 25% of the total profit.

Choice D ($750,000) would be made if you incorrectly multiplied the total profit reduction (75%) by $1,000,000. However, the question asks for the profit, not the profit reduction.

7. Both *indeterminate* and *inconclusive* mean *vague* and *indefinite,* so Choice D is correct. Choice A is incorrect, because the word *ineluctable* means inescapable or inevitable. The reading passage does not support the conclusion that the research results are incorrect or unreasonable, so Choice B and Choice C can be eliminated from consideration.

8. Choice D is correct. The reading passage states, *The sales were phenomenal, and there is a great demand for more Futuron to be manufactured. The profits to be made by increasing the manufacturing and sale of Futuron could place the Smith Paint Company in a leading role in the paint industry.* Since the sales of Futuron were phenomenal (remarkable; extraordinary), and there still is a great demand for it, the suggestion of considerable future profit is reasonable.

Choice A is not the most accurate conclusion based on the reading passage. The financial impact of decreasing the production of the traditional paint cannot be ascertained. Therefore, it is not certain that the proposed 50% reduction in the manufacturing of the Smith Paint Company's traditional paint would not financially injure that company. Certainly, Choice D is a more accurate conclusion.

Choice B is incorrect. A greater proportion of the employees being in favor of the proposed increase in Futuron production than not being in favor of it implies that over 50% of the employees are in favor of it. However, the reading passage states that most of the employees (which, logically, means over 50% of the employees) do not want the proposed change to occur.

Choice C also is not the most accurate conclusion. It states that the proposed increase in Futuron production would cause employees considerable health damage. The reading passage is not definite on this issue of health damage. It states, *Initial research indicates that negative physical reactions may result from working closely with the chemicals necessary....* How serious the health damage might be is not stated in the reading passage.

ARITHMETIC
EXAMINATION SECTION
TEST 1

DIRECTIONS: Each question or incomplete statement is followed by several suggested answers or completions. Select the one that BEST answers the question or completes the statement. PRINT THE LETTER OF TEE CORRECT ANSWER IN THE SPACE AT THE RIGHT.

1. Add $4.34, $34.50, $6.00, $101.76, $90.67. From the result, subtract $60.54 and $10,56.   1._____
   A. $76.17   B. $156.37   C. $166.17   D. $300.37

2. Add 2,200, 2,600, 252 and 47.96. From the result, subtract 202.70, 1,200, 2,150 and 434.43.   2._____
   A. 1,112.83   B. 1,213.46   C. 1,341.51   D. 1,348.91

3. Multiply 1850 by .05 and multiply 3300 by .08 and, then, add both results,   3._____
   A. 242.50   B. 264,00   C. 333.25   D. 356.50

4. Multiply 312.77 by .04. Round off the result to the nearest hundredth.   4._____
   A. 12.52   B. 12.511   C. 12.518   D. 12.51

5. Add 362.05, 91.13, 347.81 and 17.46 and then divide the result by 6. The answer, rounded off to the nearest hundredth, is: 5._____
   A. 138.409   B. 137.409   C. 136.41   D. 136.40

6. Add 66.25 and 15.06 and, then, multiply the result by 2 1/6. The answer is, most nearly,   6._____
   A. 176.18   B. 176.17   C. 162.66   D. 162.62

7. Each of the following items contains three decimals. In which case do all three decimals have the SAME value?   7._____
   A. .3; .30; .03
   C. 1.9; 1.90;1.09
   B. .25; .250; .2500
   D. .35; .350; .035

8. Add 1/2 the sum of (539.84 and 479.26) to 1/3 the sum of (1461.93 and 927.27). Round off the result to the nearest whole number.   8._____
   A. 3408   B. 2899   C. 1816   D. 1306

9. Multiply $5,906.09 by 15% and, then, divide the result by 3 and round off to the nearest cent.   9._____
   A. $295.30   B. $885.91   C. $2,657.74   D. $29,530.45

10. Multiply 630 by 517.   10._____
    A. 325,710   B. 345,720   C. 362,425   D. 385,660

2 (#1)

11. Multiply 35 by 846. 11._____
    A. 4050   B. 9450   C. 18740   D. 29610

12. Multiply 823 by 0.05. 12._____
    A. 0.4115   B. 4.115   C. 41.15   D. 411.50

13. Multiply 1690 by 0.10. 13._____
    A. 0.169   B. .1.69   C. 16.90   D. 169.0

14. Divide 2765 by 35. 14._____
    A. 71   B. 79   C. 87   D. 93

15. From $18.55 subtract $6.80. 15._____
    A. $9.75   B. $10.95   C. $11.75   D. $25.35

16. The sum of 2.75 + 4.50 + 3.60 is: 16._____
    A. 9.75   B. 10.85   C. 11.15   D. 11.95

17. The sum of 9.63 + 11.21 + 17.25 is: 17._____
    A. 36.09   B. 38.09   C. 39.92   D. 41.22

18. The sum of 112.0 + 16.9 + 3.84 is: 18._____
    A. 129.3   B. 132.74   C. 136.48   D. 167.3

19. When 65 is added to the result of 14 multiplied by 13, the answer is: 19._____
    A. 92   B. 182   C. 247   D. 16055

20. From $391.55 subtract $273.45. 20._____
    A. $118.10   B. $128.20   C. $178.10   D. $218.20

KEY (CORRECT ANSWERS)

1.	C		11.	D
2.	A		12.	C
3.	D		13.	D
4.	D		14.	B
5.	C		15.	C
6.	B		16.	B
7.	B		17.	B
8.	D		18.	B
9.	C		19.	C
10.	A		20.	A

SOLUTIONS TO PROBLEMS

1. ($4.34 + $34.50 + $6.00 + $101.76 + $90.67) - ($60.54 + $10.56) = $237.27 - $71.10 = $166.17.

2. (2200 + 2600 + 252 + 47.96) - (202.70 + 1200 + 2150 + 434.43) = 5099.96 - 3987.13 = 1112.83

3. (1850)(.05) + (3300)(.08) = 92.5 + 264 = 356.50

4. (312.77)(.04) = 12.5108 = 12.51 to nearest hundredth

5. $(362.05 + 91.13 + 347.81 + 17.46) \div 6 = 136.408\overline{3} = 136.41$ to nearest hundredth

6. $(66.25 + 15.06)(2\frac{1}{6}) = 176.17\overline{16} \approx 176.17$

7. .25 = .250 = .2500

8. $(\frac{1}{2})(539.84 + 479.26) + \frac{1}{3}(1461.93 + 927.27) = 509.55 + 796.4 = 1305.95 = 1306$ nearest whole number

9. ($5906.09)(.15) ÷ 3 = ($885.9135)/3 = 295.3045 = $295.30 to nearest cent

10. (630)(517) = 325,710

11. (35)(846) = 29,610

12. (823)(.05) = 41.15

13. (1690)(10) = 169.0

14. 2765 ÷ 3.5 = 79

15. $18.55 - $6.80 = $11.75

16. 2.75 + 4.50 + 3.60 = 10.85

17. 9.63 + 11.21 + 17.25 = 38.09

18. 112.0 + 16.9 + 3.84 = 132.74

19. 65 + (14)(13) = 65 + 182 = 247

20. $391.55 - $273.45 = $118.10

TEST 2

DIRECTIONS: Each question or incomplete statement is followed by several suggested answers or completions. Select the one that *BEST* answers the question or completes the statement. *PRINT THE LETTER OF TEE CORRECT ANSWER IN THE SPACE AT THE RIGHT.*

1. The sum of $29.61 + $101.53 + $943.64 is: 1.____
    A. $983.88   B. $1074.78   C. $1174.98   D. $1341.42

2. The sum of $132.25 + $85.63 + $7056,44 is: 2.____
    A. $1694.19   B. $7274.32   C. $8464.57   D. $9346.22

3. The sum of 4010 + 1271 + 838 + 23 is: 3.____
    A. 6142   B. 6162   C. 6242   D. 6362

4. The sum of 53632 + 27403 + 98765 + 75424 is: 4.____
    A. 19214   B. 215214   C. 235224   D. 255224

5. The sum of 76342 + 49050 + 21206 + 59989 is: 5.____
    A. 196586   B. 206087   C. 206587   D. 234487

6. The sum of $452.13 + $963.45 + $621.25 is: 6.____
    A. $1936.83   B. $2036.83   C. $2095.73   D. $2135.73

7. The sum of 36392 + 42156 + 98765 is: 7.____
    A. 167214   B. 177203   C. 177313   D. 178213

8. The sum of 40125 + 87123 + 24689 is: 8.____
    A. 141827   B. 151827   C. 151937   D. 161947

9. The sum of 2379 + 4015 + 6521 + 9986 is: 9.____
    A. 22901   B. 22819   C. 21801   D. 21791

10. From 50962 subtract 36197. 10.____
    A. 14675   B. 14765   C. 14865   D. 24765

11. From 90000 subtract 31928. 11.____
    A. 58072   B. 59062   C. 68172   D. 69182

12. From 63764 subtract 21548. 12.____
    A. 42216   B. 43122   C. 45126   D. 85312

13. From $9605.13 subtract $2715.96. 13.____
    A. $12,321.09   B. $8,690.16   C. $6,990.07   D. $6,889.17

14. From 76421 subtract 73101.   14.____
    A. 3642   B. 3540   C. 3320   D. 3242

15. From $8.25 subtract $6.50.   15.____
    A. $1.25   B. $1.50   C. $1.75   D. $2.25

16. Multiply 583 by 0.50.   16.____
    A. $291.50   B. 28.15   C. 2.815   D. 0.2815

17. Multiply 0.35 by 1045.   17.____
    A. 0.36575   B. 3.6575   C. 36.575   D. 365.75

18. Multiply 25 by 2513.   18.____
    A. 62825   B. 62725   C. 60825   D. 52825

19. Multiply 423 by 0.01.   19.____
    A. 0.0423   B. 0.423   C. 4.23   D. 42.3

20. Multiply 6.70 by 3.2.   20.____
    A. 2.1440   B. 21.440   C. 214.40   D. 2144.0

KEY (CORRECT ANSWERS)

1.	B	11.	A
2.	B	12.	A
3.	A	13.	D
4.	D	14.	C
5.	C	15.	C
6.	B	16.	A
7.	C	17.	D
8.	C	18.	A
9.	A	19.	C
10.	B	20.	B

SOLUTIONS TO PROBLEMS

1. $29.61 + $101.53 + $943.64 = $1074.78
2. $132.25 + $85.63 + $7056.44 = $7274.32
3. 4010 + 1271 + 838 + 23 = 6142
4. 53,632 + 27,403 + 98,765 + 75,424 = 255,224
5. 76,342 + 49,050 + 21,206 + 59,989 = 206,587
6. $452.13 + $963.45 + $621.25 = $2036.83
7. 36,392 + 42,156 + 98,765 = 177,313
8. 40,125 + 87,123 + 24,689 = 151,937
9. 2379 + 4015 + 6521 + 9986 = 22,901
10. 50962 - 36197 = 14,765
11. 90,000 - 31,928 = 58,072
12. 63,764 - 21,548 = 42,216
13. $9605.13 - $2715.96 = $6889.17
14. 76,421 - 73,101 = 3320
15. $8.25 - $6.50 = $1.75
16. (583)(.50) = 291.50
17. (.35)(1045) = 365.75
18. (25)(2513) = 62,825
19. (423)(.01) = 4.23
20. (6.70)(3.2) = 21.44

TEST 3

DIRECTIONS: Each question or incomplete statement is followed by several suggested answers or completions. Select the one that BEST answers the question or completes the statement. PRINT THE LETTER OF TEE CORRECT ANSWER IN THE SPACE AT THE RIGHT.

Questions 1-4.

DIRECTIONS: For each of Questions 1-4, perform the indicated arithmetic and choose the correct answer from among the four choices given.

1. 12.485
   + 347

   A. 12,038   B. 12,128   C. 12,782   D. 12,832

   1.____

2. 74,137
   + 711

   A. 74,326   B. 74,848   C. 78,028   D. .D. 78,926

   2.____

3. 3,749
   - 671

   A. 3,078   B. 3,168   C. 4,028   D. 4,420

   3.____

4. 19,805
   -18904

   A. 109   B. 901   C. 1,109   D. 1,901

   4.____

5. When 119 is subtracted from the sum of 2016 + 1634, the remainder is:

   A. 2460   B. 3531   C. 3650   D. 3769

   5.____

6. Multiply 35 X 65 X 15.

   A. 2275   B. 24265   C. 31145   D. 34125

   6.____

7. 90% expressed as a decimal is:

   A. .009   B. .09   C. .9   D. 9.0

   7.____

8. Seven-tenths of a foot expressed in inches is:

   A. 5.5   B. 6.5   C. 7   D. 8.4

   8.____

9. If 95 men were divided into crews of five men each, the *number* of crews that will be formed is:

   A. 16   B. 17   C. 18   D. 19

   9.____

10. If a man earns $19.50 an hour, the *number* of working hours it will take him to earn $4,875 is, most nearly,

   A. 225   B. 250   C. 275   D. 300

11. If 5 1/2 loads of gravel cost $55.00, then 6 1/2 loads will cost:

   A. $60.   B. $62.50   C. $65.   D. $66.00

12. At $2.50 a yard, 27 yards of concrete will cost:

   A. $36.   B. $41.80   C. $54.   D. $67.50

13. A distance is measured and found to be 52.23 feet. In feet and inches, this distance is, most nearly, 52 feet *and*

   A. 2 3/4"   B. 3 1/4"   C. 3 3/4"   D. 4 1/4"

14. If a maintainer gets $5.20 per hour and time and one-half for working over 40 hours, his *gross* salary for a week in which he worked 43 hours would be

   A. $208.00   B. $223.60   C. $231.40   D. $335.40

15. The circumference of a circle is given by the formula $C = \Pi D$, where C is the circumference, D is the diameter, and Π is about 3 1/7.
    If a coil is 15 turns of steel cable has an average diameter of 20 inches, the *total* length of cable on the coil is *nearest to*

   A. 5 feet   B. 78 feet   C. 550 feet   D. 943 feet

16. The measurements of a poured concrete foundation show that 54 cubic feet of concrete have been placed.
    If payment for this concrete is to be on the basis of cubic yards, the 54 cubic feet must be

   A. multiplied by 27   B. multiplied by 3
   C. divided by 27   D. divided by 3

17. If the cost of 4 1/2 tons of structural steel is $1,800, then the cost of 12 tons is, most nearly,

   A. $4,800   B. $5,400   C. $7,200   D. $216,000

18. An hourly-paid employee working 12:00 midnight to 8:00 a.m. is directed to report to the medical staff for a physical examination at 11:00 a.m. of the same day.
    The pay allowed him for reporting will be an extra

   A. 1 hour   B. 2 hours   C. 3 hours   D. 4 hours

19. The *total* length of four pieces of 2" pipe, whose lengths are 7' 3 1/2", 4' 2 3/16", 5' 7 5/16", and 8' 5 7/8", respectively, is:

   A. 24' 6 3/4"   B. 24' 7 15/16"
   C. 25' 5 13/16"   D. 25' 6 7/8"

3 (#3)

20. As a senior mortuary caretaker, you are preparing a monthly report, using the following figures: 20.____

    No. of bodies received   983
    No. of bodies claimed   720
    No. of bodies sent to city cemetery   14
    No. of bodies sent to medical schools   9

How many bodies remained at the end of the monthly reporting period?

  A. 230   B. 240   C. 250   D. 260

KEY (CORRECT ANSWERS)

1.	D	11.	C
2.	B	12.	D
3.	A	13.	A
4.	B	14.	C
5.	B	15.	B
6.	D	16.	C
7.	C	17.	A
8.	D	18.	C
9.	D	19.	D
10.	B	20.	B

SOLUTIONS TO PROBLEMS

1. 12,485 + 347 = 12,832

2. 74,137 + 711 = 74,848

3. 3749 - 671 = 3078

4. 19,805 - 18,904 = 901

5. (2016 + 1634) - 119 = 3650 - 119 = 3531

6. (35)(65)(15) = 34,125

7. 90% = .90 or .9

8. $(\frac{7}{10})(12) = 8.4$ inches

9. 95 ÷ 5 = 19 crews

10. $4875 ÷ $19.50 = 250 days

11. Let x = cost. Then, $\frac{5\frac{1}{2}}{6\frac{1}{2}} = \frac{\$55.00}{x}$. $5\frac{1}{2} = 357.50$. Solving, x = $65

12. ($2.50)(27) = $67.50

13. .23-ft. = 2.76 in., so 52.23 ft ≈ 52 ft. $2\frac{3}{4}$ in. $(.76 \approx \frac{3}{4})$

14. Salary = ($5.20)(40) + ($7.80)(3) = $231.40

15. Length ≈ $(15)(3\frac{1}{7})(20)$ ≈ 943 in. ≈ 78 ft.

16. There are 27 cu.ft. in 1 cu.yd. To change from 54 cu.ft. to cu.yds., divide by 27.

17. $1800 ÷ $4\frac{1}{2}$ = = $400 per ton. Then, 12 tons cost ($400)(12) = $4800

18. Instead of working 12 to 8, he will be staying until 11 AM, an extra 3 hours.

19. $7'3\frac{1}{2}" + 4'2\frac{3}{16}" + 5'7\frac{5}{16}" + 8'5\frac{7}{8}" = 24'17\frac{30}{16}" = 24'18\frac{7}{8}"$

20. 983 - 720 - 14 - 9 = 240 bodies left.

ARITHMETICAL COMPUTATION AND REASONING
EXAMINATION SECTION
TEST 1

DIRECTIONS: Each question or incomplete statement is followed by several suggested answers or completions. Select the one that BEST answers the question or completes the statement. *PRINT THE LETTER OF THE CORRECT ANSWER IN THE SPACE AT THE RIGHT.*

1. 3/8 less than $40 is   1._____
   A. $25   B. $65   C. $15   D. $55

2. 27/64 expressed as a percent is   2._____
   A. 40.625%   B. 42.188%   C. 43.750%   D. 45.313%

3. 1/6 more than 36 gross is _____ gross.   3._____
   A. 6   B. 48   C. 30   D. 42

4. 15 is 20% of   4._____

5. The number which when increased by 1/3 of itself equals 96 is   5._____
   A. 128   B. 72   C. 64   D. 32

6. 0.16 3/4 written as percent is   6._____
   A. 16 3/4%   B. 16.3/4%   C. .016 3/4%   D. .0016 3/4%

7. 55% of 15 is   7._____
   A. 82.5   B. 0.825   C. 0.0825   D. 8.25

8. The number which when decreased by 1/3 of itself equals 96 is   8._____
   A. 64   B. 32   C. 128   D. 144

9. A carpenter used a board 15 3/4 ft. long from which 3 footstools were made with sufficient lumber left over for half of another footstool. If the lumber cost 24 1/2¢ per foot, the cost of EACH footstool was   9._____
   A. $1.54   B. $3.86   C. $1.10   D. $1.08

10. In one year, a luncheonette purchased 1231 gallons of milk for $907.99. The AVERAGE cost per half pint was   10._____
    A. $0.046   B. $0.045   C. $0.047   D. $0.044

11. The product of 23 and 9 3/4 is   11._____
    A. 191 2/3   B. 224 1/4   C. 213 3/4   D. 32 3/4

12. An order for 345 machine bolts at $4.15 per hundred will cost   12._____
    A. $0.1432   B. $1.1432   C. $14.32   D. $143.20

2 (#1)

13. The fractional equivalent of .0625 is 13._____
 A. 1/16 B. 1/15 C. 1/14 D. 1/13

14. The number 0.03125 equals 14._____
 A. 3/64 B. 1/16 C. 1/64 D. 1/32

15. 21.70 divided by 1.75 equals 15._____
 A. 124 B. 12.4 C. 1.24 D. .124

16. The average cost of school lunches for 100 children varied as follows: Monday, $0.285; 16._____
 Tuesday, $0.237; Wednesday, $0.264; Thursday, $0.276; Friday, $0.292.
 The AVERAGE lunch cost
 A. $0.136 B. $0.270 C. $0.135 D. $0.271

17. The cost of 5 dozen eggs at $8.52 per gross is 17._____
 A. $3.50 B. $42.60 C. $3.55 D. $3.74

18. 410.07 less 38.49 equals 18._____
 A. 372.58 B. 371.58 C. 381.58 D. 382.68

19. The cost of 7 3/4 tons of coal at $20.16 per ton is 19._____
 A. $15.12 B. $151.20 C. $141.12 D. $156.24

20. The sum of 90.79, 79.09, 97.90, and 9.97 is 20._____
 A. 277.75 B. 278.56 C. 276.94 D. 277.93

KEY (CORRECT ANSWERS)

1. A   11. B
2. B   12. C
3. D   13. A
4. C   14. D
5. B   15. B

6. A   16. D
7. D   17. C
8. D   18. B
9. C   19. D
10. A 20. A

SOLUTIONS TO PROBLEMS

1. ($40)(5/8) = $25

2. 27/64 = .421875 ≈ 42.188%

3. (36)(1 1/6) = 42

4. Let x = missing number. Then, 15 = .20x. Solving, x = 75

5. Let x = missing number. Then, x + 1/3 x = 96. Simplifying, 4/3 x = 96. Solving, x = 96 ÷ 4/3 = 72

6. .16 3/4 = 16 3/4% by simply moving the decimal point two places to the right.

7. (.55)(15) = 8.25

8. Let x = missing number. Then, x - 1/3 x = 96. Simplifying, 2/3 x = 96. Solving, x = 96 ÷ 2/3 = 144

9. 15 3/4 ÷ 3 1/2 = 4.5 feet per footstool. The cost of one footstool is ($.245)(4.5) = $1.1025 ≈ $1.10

10. $907.99 ÷ 1231 = $.7376 per gallon. Since there are 16 half-pints in a gallon, the average cost per half-pint is $.7376 ÷ 16 ≈ $.046

11. (23)(9 3/4) = (23)(9.75) = 224.25 or 224 1/4

12. ($4.15)(3.45) = $14.3175 = $14.32

13. .0625 = 625/10,000 = 1/16

14. .03125 = 3125/100,000 = 1/32

15. 21.70 ÷ 1.75 = 12.4

16. The sum of these lunches is $1.354. Then, $1.354 ÷ 5 = $.2708 = $.271

17. $8.52 ÷ 12 = $.71 per dozen. Then, the cost of 5 dozen is ($.71)(5) = $3.55

18. 410.07 - 38.49 = 371.58

19. ($20.16)(7.75) = $156.24

20. 90.79 + 79.09 + 97.90 + 9.97 = 277.75

TEST 2

DIRECTIONS: Each question or incomplete statement is followed by several suggested answers or completions. Select the one that BEST answers the question or completes the statement. *PRINT THE LETTER OF THE CORRECT ANSWER IN THE SPACE AT THE RIGHT.*

1. 1600 is 40% of what number?

    A. 6400   B. 3200   C. 4000   D. 5600

    1._____

2. An executive's time card reads: Arrived 9:15 A.M., Left 2:05 P.M. How many hours was he in the office? _____ hours _____ minutes.

    A. 5; 10   B. 4; 50   C. 4; 10   D. 5; 50

    2._____

3. .4266 times .3333 will have the following number of decimals in the product:

    A. 8   B. 4   C. 1   D. None of these

    3._____

4. An office floor is 25 ft. wide by 36 ft. long. To cover this floor with carpet will require _____ square yards.

    A. 100   B. 300   C. 900   D. 25

    4._____

5. 1/8 of 1% expressed as a decimal is

    A. .125   B. .0125   C. 1.25   D. .00125

    5._____

6. $\dfrac{6 \div 4}{6 \times 4}$ equals 6x4

    A. 1/16   B. 1   C. 1/6   D. 1/4

    6._____

7. 1/25 of 230 equals

    A. 92.0   B. 9.20   C. .920   D. 920

    7._____

8. 4 times 3/8 equals

    A. 1 3/8   B. 3/32   C. 12.125   D. 1.5

    8._____

9. 3/4 divided by 4 equals

    A. 3   B. 3/16   C. 16/3   D. 16

    9._____

10. 6/7 divided by 2/7 equals

    A. 6   B. 12/49   C. 3   D. 21

    10._____

11. The interest on $240 for 90 days ' 6% is

    A. $4.80   B. $3.40   C. $4.20   D. $3.60

    11._____

12. 16 2/3% of 1728 is

    A. 91   B. 288   C. 282   D. 280

    12._____

2 (#2)

13. 6 1/4% of 6400 is   13.____
    A. 2500   B. 410   C. 108   D. 400

14. 12 1/2% of 560 is   14.____
    A. 65   B. 40   C. 50   D. 70

15. 2 yards divided by 3 equals   15.____
    A. 2 feet   B. 1/2 yard   C. 3 yards   D. 3 feet

16. A school has 540 pupils. 45% are boys. How many girls are there in this school?   16.____
    A. 243   B. 297   C. 493   D. 394

17. .1875 is equivalent to   17.____
    A. 18 3/4   B. 75/18   C. 18/75   D. 3/16

18. A kitchen cabinet listed at $42 is sold for $33.60. The discount allowed is   18.____
    A. 10%   B. 15%   C. 20%   D. 30%

19. 3 6/8 divided by 8 1/4 equals   19.____
    A. 9 1/8   B. 12   C. 5/11   D. 243.16

20. An agent sold goods to the amount of $1480. His commission at 5 1/2% was   20.____
    A. $37.50   B. $81.40   C. 76.70   D. $81.10

KEY (CORRECT ANSWERS

1. C   11. D
2. B   12. B
3. A   13. D
4. A   14. D
5. D   15. A

6. A   16. B
7. B   17. D
8. D   18. C
9. B   19. C
10. C   20. B

SOLUTIONS TO PROBLEMS

1. Let x = missing number. Then, 1600 = .40x. Solving, x = 4000
2. 2:05 PM - 9:15 AM = 4 hours 50 minutes
3. The product of two 4-decimal numbers is an 8-decimal number.
4. (25 ft)(36 ft) = 900 sq.ft. = 100 sq.yds.
5. (1/8)(1%) = (.125)(.01) = .00125
6. (6 ÷ 4) ÷ (6 x 4) = 3/2 ÷ 24 = (3/2)(1/24) = (1/16)
7. (1/25)(230) = 9.20
8. (4)(3/8) = 12/8 = 1.5
9. 3/4 ÷ 4 = (3/4)(1/4) = 3/16
10. 6/7 / 2/7 = (6/7)(7/2) = 3
11. ($240)(.06)(90/360) = $3.60
12. (16 2/3%)(1728) = (1/6)(1728) = 288
13. (6 1/4%)(6400) = (1/16)(6400) = 400
14. (12 1/2%)(560) = (1/8)(560) = 70
15. 2 yds ÷ 3 = 2/3 yds = (2/3)(3) = 2 ft.
16. If 45% are boys, then 55% are girls. Thus, (540)(.55) = 297
17. .1875 = 1875/10,000 = 3/16
18. $42 - $33.60 = $8.40.
    The discount is $8.40 ÷ $42 = .20 = 20%
19. 3 6/8 - 8 1/4 = (30/8)(4/33) = 5/11
20. ($1480)(.055) = $81.40

TEST 3

DIRECTIONS: Each question or incomplete statement is followed by several suggested answers or completions. Select the one that BEST answers the question or completes the statement. *PRINT THE LETTER OF THE CORRECT ANSWER IN THE SPACE AT THE RIGHT.*

1. 93.648 divided by 0.4 is

    A. 23.412　　B. 234.12　　C. 2.3412　　D. 2341.2

    1.____

2. Add 4.3682, .0028, 34., 9.92, and from the sum subtract 1.992. The remainder is

    A. .46299　　B. 4.6299　　C. 462.99　　D. 46.299

    2.____

3. At $2.88 per gross, three dozen will cost

    A. $8.64　　B. $0.96　　C. $0.72　　D. $11.52

    3.____

4. 13 times 2.39 times 0.024 equals

    A. 745.68　　B. 74.568　　C. 7.4568　　D. .74568

    4.____

5. A living room suite is marked $64 less 25 percent. A cash discount of 10 percent is allowed. The cash price is

    A. $53.20　　B. $47.80　　C. $36.00　　D. $43.20

    5.____

6. 1/8 of 1 percent expressed as a decimal is

    A. .125　　B. .0125　　C. 1.25　　D. .00125

    6.____

7. 16 percent of 482.11 equals

    A. 77.1376　　B. 771.4240　　C. 7714.2400　　D. 7.71424

    7.____

8. A merchant sold a chair for $60. This was at a profit of 25 percent of what it cost him. The chair cost him

    A. $48　　B. $45　　C. $15　　D. $75

    8.____

9. Add 5 hours 13 minutes, 3 hours 49 minutes, and 14 minutes. The sum is _____ hours _____ minutes.

    A. 9; 16　　B. 9; 76　　C. 8; 16　　D. 8; 6

    9.____

10. 89 percent of $482 is

    A. $428.98　　B. $472.36　　C. $42.90　　D. $47.24

    10.____

11. 200 percent of 800 is

    A. 16　　B. 1600　　C. 2500　　D. 4

    11.____

12. Add 2 feet 3 inches, 4 feet 11 inches, 8 inches, 6 feet 6 inches. The sum is _____ feet _____ inches.

    A. 12; 4　　B. 12; 14　　C. 14; 4　　D. 14; 28

    12.____

13. A merchant bought dresses at $15 each and sold them at $20 each. His overhead expenses are 20 percent of cost. His net profit on each dress is   13.____

    A. $1 B. $2 C. $3 D. $4

14. 0.0325 expressed as a percent is   14.____

    A. 325% B. 3 1/4% C. 32 1/2% D. 32.5%

15. Add 3/4, 1/8, 1/32, 1/2; and from the sum subtract 4/8. The remainder is   15.____

    A. 2/32 B. 7/8 C. 29/32 D. 3/4

16. A salesman gets a commission of 4 percent on his sales. If he wants his commission to amount to $40, he will have to sell merchandise totaling   16.____

    A. $160 B. $10 C. $1,000 D. $100

17. Jones borrowed $225,000 for five years at 3 1/2 percent. The annual interest charge was   17.____

    A. $1,575 B. $1,555 C. $7,875 D. $39,375

18. A kitchen cabinet listed at $42 is sold for $33.60. The discount allowed is _____ percent.   18.____

    A. 10 B. 15 C. 20 D. 30

19. The exact number of days from May 5, 2007 to July 1, 2007 is _____ days.   19.____

    A. 59 B. 58 C. 56 D. 57

20. A dealer sells an article at a loss of 50% of the cost. Based on the selling price, the loss is   20.____

    A. 25% B. 50% C. 100% D. none of these

KEY (CORRECT ANSWERS)

1.	B	11.	B
2.	D	12.	C
3.	C	13.	B
4.	D	14.	B
5.	D	15.	C
6.	D	16.	C
7.	A	17.	C
8.	A	18.	C
9.	A	19.	D
10.	A	20.	C

3 (#3)

SOLUTIONS TO PROBLEMS

1. $93.648 \div .4 = 234.12$

2. $4.368 + .0028 + 34 + 9.92 - 1.992 = 48.291 - 1.992 = 46.299$

3. $2.88 for 12 dozen means $.24 per dozen. Three dozen will cost (3)($.24) = $.72

4. $(13)(2.39)(.024) = .74568$

5. $(\$64)(.75)(.90) = \$43.20$

6. $(1/8)(1\%) = (.125)(.01) = .00125$

7. $(.16)(482.11) = 77.1376$

8. Let x = cost. Then, $1.25x = \$60$. Solving, $x = \$48$

9. 5 hrs. 13 min. + 3 hrs. 49 min. + 14 min = 8 hrs. 76 min.

10. $(.89)(\$482) = \$428.98$

11. $200\% = 2$. So, $(200\%)(800) = (2)(800) = 1600$

12. 2 ft. 3 in. + 4 ft. 11 in. + 8 in. + 6 ft. 6 in. + 12 ft. 28 in. = 14 ft. 4 in.

13. Overhead is $(.20)(\$15) = \$3$. The net profit is $\$20 - \$15 - \$3 = \$2$

14. $.0325 = 3.25\% = 3\ 1/4\%$

15. $3/4 + 1/8 + 1/32 + 1/2 - 4/8 = 45/32 - 4/8 = 29/32$

16. Let x = sales. Then, $\$40 = .04x$. Solving, $x = \$1000$

17. Annual interest is $(\$225,000)(.035) \times 1 = 7875$

18. $\$42 - \$33.60 = \$8.40$. Then, $\$8.40 \div \$42 = .20 = 20\%$

19. The number of days left for May, June, July is 26, 30, and 1. Thus, $26 + 30 + 1 = 57$

20. Let x = cost, so that $.50x$ = selling price. The loss is represented by $.50x \div .50x = 1 = 100\%$ on the selling price. (Note: The loss in dollars is $x - .50x = .50x$)

ARITHMETICAL REASONING

EXAMINATION SECTION
TEST 1

DIRECTIONS: Each question or incomplete statement is followed by several suggested answers or completions. Select the one that BEST answers the question or completes the statement. *PRTNT THE LETTER OF THE CORRECT ANSWER IN THE SPACE AT THE RIGHT.*

1. Assume that it takes approximately 1 1/2 minutes to unload a dozen identical items from a delivery truck.
   At this speed, the *amount* of time it should take to unload a shipment of 876 items is, most nearly,_____ minutes.

   A. 9Q   B. 100   C. 110   D. 120

   1.____

2. Assume that a shop clerk has received a bill of $108 for a delivery of clamps which cost $4.32 per dozen.
   How many clamps should there be in this delivery?

   A. 25   B. 36   C. 300   D. 360

   2.____

3. Employee A has not used any leave time and has accumulated a total of 45 leave-days. How many months did it take employee A to have accumulated 45 leave-days if the accrual rate is 1 2/3 days per month?

   A. 25   B. 27   C. 29   D. 31

   3.____

4. A shop clerk is notified that only 75 bolts can be supplied by Vendor A.
   If this represents 12.5% of the total requisition, then how many bolts were originally ordered?

   A. 125   B. 600   C. 700   D. 900

   4.____

5. An enclosed square-shaped storage area with sides of 16 feet each has a. safe-load capacity of 250 pounds per square foot.
   The *MAXIMUM evenly distributed* weight that can be stored in this area is_____ lbs.

   A. 1,056   B. 4,000   C. 64,000   D. 102,400

   5.____

6. A clerical employee completed 70 progress reports the first week, 87 the second week, and 80 the third week. Assuming a 4-week month, how many progress reports must the clerk complete in the fourth week in order to attain an average of 85 progress reports per week for the month?

   A. 93   B. 103   C. 113   D. 133

   6.____

7. On the first of the month, Shop X received a delivery of 150 gallons of lubricating oil. During the month, the following amounts of oil were used on lubricating work each week: 30 quarts, 36 quarts, 20 quarts, and 48 quarts.
   The amount of lubricating oil *remaining* at the end of the month was_____ gallons.

   A. 4   B. 33.5   C. 41.5   D. 116.5

   7.____

8. For working a 35-hour week, Employee A earns a gross amount of $160.30. For each hour that Employee A works over 40 hours a week, he is entitled to 1 1/2 times his hourly wage rate.
   If Employee A worked 9 hours on Monday, 8 hours on Tuesday, 9 hours 30 minutes on Wednesday, 9 hours 15 minutes on Thursday, and 9 hours 15 minutes on Friday, what should his *gross* salary be for that week?

   A. $206.10   B. $210.68   C. $217.55   D. $229.00

9. An enclosed cube-shaped storage bay has dimensions of 12 feet by 12 feet by 12 feet. Standard procedure requires that there be at least 1 foot of space between the walls, the ceiling and the stored items. What is the MAXIMUM number of cube-shaped boxes with length, width and height of 1 foot each that can be stored on 1-foot high pallets in this bay?

   A. 1,000   B. 1,331   C. 1,452   D. 1,728

10. Assume that two ceilings are to be painted. One ceiling measures 30 feet by 15 feet and the second 45 feet by 60 feet. If one quart of paint will cover 60 square feet of ceiling, approximately how much paint will be required to paint the two ceilings?

    A. 6 gallons   B. 10 gallons   C. 13 gallons   D. 18 gallons

KEY (CORRECT ANSWER)

1. C
2. C
3. B
4. B
5. C

6. B
7. D
8. C
9. A
10. C

3 (#1)

SOLUTIONS TO PROBLEMS

1. 876 ÷ 12 = 73. Then, (73)(1 1/2) = 109.5 ≈ 110 minutes.

2. $108 ÷ $4.32 = 25. Then, (25)(12) = 300 clamps.

3. 45 ÷ 1 1/2 = 27 months.

4. 75 ÷ .125 = 600 bolts

5. (16)(16)(250) = 64,000 pounds

6. (85)(4) = 340. Then, 340 - 70 - 87 - 80 = 103 progress reports

7. Changing every calculation to gallons, the amount of oil remaining is 150 - 7.5 - 9 - 5 - 12 = 116.5

8. 9 + 8 + 9.5 + 9.25 + 9.25 = 45 hours. His gross pay will be ($4.58)(40) + ($6.87)(5) = $217.55. (Note: To get his regular hourly wages, divide $160.30 by 35.)

9. 12 - 1 - 1 = 10. Maximum number of boxes is $(10)^3$ = 1000

10. First ceiling contains (30)(15) = 450 sq.ft., whereas the second ceiling contains (45)(60) = 2700 sq.ft. The total sq.ft. = 3150. Now, 3150 60 = 52.5 quarts of paint = 13.125 13 gallons.

TEST 2

DIRECTIONS: Each question or incomplete statement is followed by several suggested answers or completions. Select the one that *BEST* answers the question or completes the statement. *PRTNT THE LETTER OF THE CORRECT ANSWER IN THE SPACE AT THE RIGHT.*

1. A piping sketch is drawn to a scale of 1/8" = 1 foot.
   A vertical steam line measuring 34" on the sketch would have an *actual* length of_____ feet.

   A. 16 B. 22 C. 24 D. 28

   1.___

2. Three lengths of pipe 1' 10", 3' 2 1/2", and 5' 7 1/2", respectively, are to be cut from a pipe 14' 0" long.
   Allowing 1/8" for each pipe cut, the length of pipe *remaining* is

   A. 3' 1 1/8" B. 3' 2 1/2" C. 3' 3 1/2" D. 3' 3 5/8"

   2.___

3. Assume that a steamfitter's helper earns $11.16 an hour and that he works 250 seven-hour days a year. His *gross* yearly salary will be

   A. $19,430 B. $19,530 C. $19,650 D. $19,780

   3.___

4. A pipe having an inside diameter of 3.48 inches and a wall thickness of .18 inches, will have an *outside* diameter of _____ inches.

   A. 3.84 B. 3.64 C. 3.57 D. 3.51

   4.___

5. A rectangular steel bar having a volume of 30 cubic inches, a width of 2 inches, and a height of 3 inches will have a *length* of_____ inches,

   A. 12 B. 10 C. 8 D. 5

   5.___

6. A pipe weighs 20.4 pounds per foot of length. The *total* weight of eight pieces of this pipe with each piece 20 feet in length is, most nearly, _____ pounds.

   A. 460 B. 1680 C. 2420 D. 3260

   6.___

7. In last year's budget, $7,500 was spent for office supplies. Of this amount, 60% was spent for paper supplies. If the price of paper has risen 20% over last year's price, then the *amount* that will be spent this year on paper supplies, assuming the same quantity will he purchased, will be

   A. $3,600 B. $5,200 C. $5,400 D. $6,000

   7.___

8. If it takes 4 painters 54 days to do a certain paint job, then the time that it should take 5 painters working at the *same* speed to do the *same* job is, most nearly_____ days.

   A. 3 1/2 B. 4 C. 4 1/2 D. 5

   8.___

9. A foreman assigns a gang foreman to supervise a job which must be completed at the end of 7 working days. The gang foreman has 8 maintainers in his gang. At the end of 3 working days, although the work has been efficiently done, the job is only one-third completed.
   In order to complete the job on time, *without* overtime, the gang foreman should request that he be given _____ more maintainers.

   A. 3 B. 4 C. 5 D. 6

   9.___

118

10. One shipment of 70 shovels costs $140. A second shipment of 130 shovels costs $208.00.
The *average* cost per shovel for *both* shipments is, most nearly,

    A. $1.60   B. $1.75   C. $2.00   D. $2.50

10.____

KEY (CORRECT ANSWER)

1. D   6. D
2. D   7. C
3. B   8. C
4. A   9. B
5. D   10. B

SOLUTIONS TO PROBLEMS

1. 3 1/2 ÷ 1/8 = 28 feet

2. 14' - 1'10" - 3'2 1/2" - 5'7 1/2" - 1/8" - 1/8" - 1/8" = 3'3 5/8"

3. (250)(7) = 1750 hours. Then, ($11.16)(1750) = $19,530

4. Outside diameter = 3.48 + .18 + .18 = 3.84 inches

5. Length is 30 ÷ 2 ÷ 3 = 5 inches.

6. (20)(8) = 160 feet. Then, (160)(20.4) = 3264 ≈ 3260 pounds

7. ($7500)(.60) = $4500. Then, ($4500)(1.20) = $5400

8. Let x = required days. Since this is an inverse ratio, 4/5 = x/5 1/2. Then, 5x = 22. Solving, x = 4.4 ≈ 4 1/2

9. (8)(3) = 24 man-days were needed to complete 1/3 of the job. Since 2/3 of the job remains, the foreman will need 48 man-days for the remaining 4 days. This requires 12 men. Since he has 8 currently, he will need 4 more workers.

10. Average cost per shovel is ($140 + $208) ÷ (70 + 130) = $1.74, which is closest to $1.75.

TEST 3

DIRECTIONS: Each question or incomplete statement is followed by several suggested answers or completions. Select the one that *BEST* answers the question or completes the statement. *PRTNT THE LETTER OF THE CORRECT ANSWER IN THE SPACE AT THE RIGHT.*

1. Assume that your warehouse received a shipment of 600 articles. A sample of 60 articles was inspected. Of this sample, one article was wholly defective and four articles were partly defective.
   On the basis of this sampling, you would expect the *total* number of *defective* articles in this shipment to be

   A. 5 B. 10 C. 40 D. 50

   1.____

2. Assume that you have been instructed to order mineral spirits as soon as the supply-on-hand falls to the level required for sixty days of issue.
   If the total amount of mineral spirits on hand is 960 gallons and you issue an average of 8 gallons of mineral spirits per day, and your warehouse works a five-day week, you will be *required* to order mineral spirits in_____ working days.

   A. 50 B. 60 C. 70 D. 80

   2.____

3. Assume that you work in a one-story warehouse where the total available floor space measures 175 feet by 140 feet. Of this floor space, one area measuring 35 feet by 75 feet is- used for storing materials handling equipment, another area measuring 10 feet by 21 feet is used for office space, and the remaining floor space is available for storage.
   The amount of floor space available for storage in this one-story warehouse is_____ square feet.

   A. 21,665 B. 21,875 C. 24,290 D. 24,500

   3.____

4. Assume that linoleum tiles measuring 9 inches by 9 inches are packed ten to a box and each box costs $3.50.
   The *cost* of buying enough linoleum tiles to cover an area measuring 15 feet by 21 feet is

   A. $98.00 B. $110.25 C. $196.00 D. $220.50

   4.____

5. The *number* of boxes measuring 3 inches by 3 inches by 3 inches that will fit into a carton measuring 2 feet by 4 feet by 4 feet is

   A. 2,048 B. 2,645 C. 7,936 D. 23,808

   5.____

6. The stock inventory card for paint, white, flat, one-gallon, has the following entries:

Date	Received	Shipped	Balance
April 12	-	25	75
April 13	50	75	
April 14	-	10	
April 15	25		
April 16		10	

   The balance on hand at the close of business on April 15 should be

   A. 40 B. 45 C. 55 D. 65

   6.____

2 (#3)

7. The cost of one dozen pieces of screening, each measuring 4 feet 6 inches by 5 feet, at $.10 per square foot is　　7.___

   A. $22.50　　B. $25.00　　C. $27.00　　D. $27.60

8. Assume that it takes an average of ten man-hours to stack four tons of a particular item. In order to stack 80 tons, the *number* of men required to complete the job in twenty hours is　　8.___

   A. 10　　B. 20　　C. 30　　D. 40

9. Assume that you are required to relocate 5,000 reams of unboxed paper using only manual labor. The average time required for one laborer to pick 12 reams, carry them to the new location, and store them properly, is ten minutes.
   In order to complete this relocation task within one working day of seven hours, the *minimum* number of laborers you should assign to this task is　　9.___

   A. 10　　B. 15　　C. 24　　D. 70

10. Assume that you receive a shipment of 9 boxes of paper towels. Each box contains 6 dozen packages. Each package contains 200 paper towels. The total cost of the shipment of boxes is $64.80. The unit of issue for paper towels is the package.
    The *unit* cost of the paper towels is　　10.___

    A. $.10　　B. $.90　　C. $1.20　　D. $7.20

KEY (CORRECT ANSWER)

1. D	6. D
2. B	7. C
3. A	8. A
4. C	9. A
5. A	10. A

SOLUTIONS TO PROBLEMS

1. Solve for x: 5/60 = x/600. Then, x = 50

2. 960 ÷ 8 = 120 days. Then, 120 - 60 = 60 days.

3. Storage area is (175)(140) - (35)(75) - (10)(21) = 21,665 sq.ft.

4. 9 x 9 = 81 sq.in. (81)(10) = 810 sq.in. of tiles cost $3.50 (15 ft)(21 ft) = (180)(252) = 45,360 sq.in. Now, 45,360 ÷ 810 = 56 boxes. Finally, (56)($3.50) = $196.

5. (2 ft)(4 ft)(4 ft) = (24 in)(48 in)(48 in) = 55,296 sq.in. Then, 55,296 / 27 = 2048 boxes.

6. Balance at end of April 13th is 75 + 50 - 75 = 50
   Balance at end of April 14th is 50 + 0 - 10 = 40
   Balance at end of April 15th is 40 + 25 - 0 = 65

7. (4 1/2)(5) = 224 sq.ft. Then, (22)($0.10) = $2.25 per piece. The cost of 12 pieces is ($2.25)(12) = $27.

8. If 10 man-hours are needed for 4 tons, then 200 man-hours are needed for 80 tons. The number of men needed to do the job in 20 hours is 200 ÷ 20 = 10.

9. 7 hours = 420 minutes and 420 ÷ 10 = 42.
   Then, (42)(12) = 504 reams transported per day for each laborer. Now, 5000 ÷ 504 ≈ 9.92, which gets rounded up to 10.

10. (9)(72) = 648 packages. Then, $64.80 ÷ 648 = $0.10.

NAME and NUMBER COMPARISONS

COMMENTARY

This test seeks to measure your ability and disposition to do a job carefully and accurately, your attention to exactness and preciseness of detail, your alertness and versatility in discerning similarities and differences between things, and your power in systematically handling written language symbols.

It is actually a test of your ability to do academic and/or clerical work, using the basic elements of verbal (qualitative) and mathematical (quantitative) learning - words and numbers.

EXAMINATION SECTION
TEST 1

DIRECTIONS: In each line across the page there are three names or numbers that are much alike. Compare the three names or numbers and decide which ones are exactly alike. *PRINT IN THE SPACE AT THE RIGHT THE LETTER:*
- A. if all THREE names or numbers are exactly ALIKE
- B. if only the FIRST and SECOND names or numbers are ALIKE
- C. if only the FIRST and THIRD names or numbers are ALIKE
- D. if only the SECOND and THIRD names or numbers are ALIKE
- E. if ALL THREE names or numbers are DIFFERENT

1. Davis Hazen   David Hozen   David Hazen   1._____
2. Lois Appel   Lois Appel   Lois Apfel   2._____
3. June Allan   Jane Allan   Jane Allan   3._____
4. 10235   10235   10235   4._____
5. 32614   32164   32614   5._____

TEST 2

1. 2395890   2395890   2395890   1._____
2. 1926341   1926347   1926314   2._____
3. E. Owens McVey   E. Owen McVey   E. Owen McVay   3._____
4. Emily Neal Rouse   Emily Neal Rowse   Emily Neal Rowse   4._____
5. H. Merritt Audubon H. Merriott Audubon H. Merritt Audubon 5._____

TEST 3

1.	6219354	6219354	6219354	1.____
2.	2312793	2312793	2312793	2.____
3.	1065407	1065407	1065047	3.____
4.	Francis Ransdell	Frances Ramsdell	Francis Ramsdell	4.____
5.	Cornelius Detwiler	Cornelius Detwiler	Cornelius Detwiler	5.____

TEST 4

1.	6452054	6452654	6542054	1.____
2.	8501268	8501268	8501286	2.____
3.	Ella Burk Newham	Ella Burk Newnham	Elena Burk Newnham	3.____
4.	Jno. K. Ravencroft	Jno. H. Ravencroft	Jno. H. Ravencoft	4.____
5.	Martin Wills Pullen	Martin Wills Pulen	Martin Wills Pullen	5.____

TEST 5

1.	3457988	3457986	3457986	1.____
2.	4695682	4695862	4695682	2.____
3.	Stricklund Kaneydy	Sticklund Kanedy	Stricklund Kanedy	3.____
4.	Joy Harlor Witner	Joy Harloe Witner	Joy Harloe Witner	4.____
5.	R.M.O. Uberroth	R.M.O. Uberroth	R.N.O. Uberroth	5.____

TEST 6

1.	1592514	1592574	1592574	1.____
2.	2010202	2010202	2010220	2.____
3.	6177396	6177936	6177396	3.____
4.	Drusilla S. Ridgeley	Drusilla S. Ridgeley	Drusilla S. Ridgeley	4.____
5.	Andrei I. Toumantzev	Andrei I. Tourmantzev	Andrei I. Toumantzov	5.____

TEST 7

1.	5261383	5261383	5261338	1.____
2.	8125690	8126690	8125609	2.____
3.	W.E. Johnston	W.E. Johnson	W.E. Johnson	3.____
4.	Vergil L. Muller	Vergil L. Muller	Vergil L. Muller	4.____
5.	Atherton R. Warde	Asheton R. Warde	Atherton P. Warde	5.____

TEST 8

1.	013469.5	023469.5	02346.95	1.____
2.	33376	333766	333766	2.____
3.	Ling-Temco-Vought	Ling-Tenco-Vought	Ling-Temco Vought	3.____
4.	Lorilard Corp.	Lorillard Corp.	Lorrilard Corp.	4.____
5.	American Agronomics Corporation	American Agronomics Corporation	American Agronomic Corporation	5.____

TEST 9

1. 436592864	436592864	436592864	1.____
2. 197765123	197755123	197755123	2.____
3. Dewaay, Cortvriendt International S.A.	Deway, Cortvriendt International S.A.	Deway, Corturiendt International S.A.	3.____
4. Crédit Lyonnais	Crèdit Lyonnais	Crèdit Lyonais	4.____
5. Algemene Bank Nederland N.V.	Algamene Bank Nederland N.V.	Algemene Bank Naderland N.V.	5.____

TEST 10

1. 00032572	0.0032572	00032522	1.____
2. 399745	399745	398745	2.____
3. Banca Privata Finanziaria S.p.A.	Banca Privata Finanzaria S.P.A.	Banca Privata Finanziaria S.P.A.	3.____
4. Eastman Dillon, Union Securities & Co.	Eastman Dillon, Union Securities Co.	Eastman Dillon, Union Securities & Co.	4.____
5. Arnhold and S. Bleichroeder, Inc.	Arnhold & S. Bleichroeder, Inc.	Arnold and S. Bleichroeder, Inc.	5.____

TEST 11

DIRECTIONS: Answer the questions below on the basis of the following instructions: For each such numbered set of names, addresses and numbers listed in Columns I and II, select your answer from the following options:
- A: The names in Columns I and II are different
- B: The addresses in Columns I and II are different
- C: The numbers in Columns I and II are different
- D: The names, addresses and numbers are identical

1. Francis Jones
   62 Stately Avenue
   96-12446

   Francis Jones
   62 Stately Avenue
   96-21446

   1.____

2. Julio Montez
   19 Ponderosa Road
   56-73161

   Julio Montez
   19 Ponderosa Road
   56-71361

   2.____

3. Mary Mitchell
   2314 Melbourne Drive
   68-92172

   Mary Mitchell
   2314 Melbourne Drive
   68-92172

   3.____

4. Harry Patterson
   25 Dunne Street
   14-33430

   Harry Patterson
   25 Dunne Street
   14-34330

   4.____

5. Patrick Murphy
   171 West Hosmer Street
   93-81214

   Patrick Murphy
   171 West Hosmer Street
   93-18214

   5.____

TEST 12

1. August Schultz
   816 St. Clair Avenue
   53-40149

   August Schultz
   816 St. Claire Avenue
   53-40149

   1.____

2. George Taft
   72 Runnymede Street
   47-04033

   George Taft
   72 Runnymede Street
   47-04023

   2.____

3. Angus Henderson
   1418 Madison Street
   81-76375

   Angus Henderson
   1418 Madison Street
   81-76375

   3.____

4. Carolyn Mazur
   12 Riven/lew Road
   38-99615

   Carolyn Mazur
   12 Rivervane Road
   38-99615

   4.____

5. Adele Russell
   1725 Lansing Lane
   72-91962

   Adela Russell
   1725 Lansing Lane
   72-91962

   5.____

TEST 13

DIRECTIONS: The following questions are based on the instructions given below. In each of the following questions, the 3-line name and address in Column I is the master-list entry, and the 3-line entry in Column II is the information to be checked against the master list.

    If there is one line that is *not* exactly alike, mark your answer A.
    If there are two lines *not* exactly alike, mark your answer B.
    If there are three lines *not* exactly alike, mark your answer C.
    If the lines *all are* exactly alike, mark your answer D.

1. Jerome A. Jackson
   1243 14th Avenue
   New York, N.Y. 10023

   Jerome A. Johnson
   1234 14th Avenue
   New York, N.Y. 10023

   1._____

2. Sophie Strachtheim
   33-28 Connecticut Ave.
   Far Rockaway, N.Y. 11697

   Sophie Strachtheim
   33-28 Connecticut Ave.
   Far Rockaway, N.Y. 11697

   2._____

3. Elisabeth NT. Gorrell
   256 Exchange St
   New York, N.Y. 10013

   Elizabeth NT. Gorrell
   256 Exchange St.
   New York, N.Y. 10013

   3._____

4. Maria J. Gonzalez
   7516 E. Sheepshead Rd.
   Brooklyn, N.Y. 11240

   Maria J. Gonzalez
   7516 N. Shepshead Rd.
   Brooklyn, N.Y. 11240

   4._____

5. Leslie B. Brautenweiler
   21-57A Seller Terr.
   Flushing, N.Y. 11367

   Leslie B. Brautenwieler
   21-75A Seiler Terr.
   Flushing, N.J. 11367

   5._____

KEYS (CORRECT ANSWERS)

TEST 1	TEST 2	TEST 3	TEST 4	TEST 5	TEST 6	TEST 7
1. E	1. A	1. A	1. E	1. D	1. D	1. B
2. B	2. E	2. A	2. B	2. C	2. B	2. E
3. D	3. E	3. B	3. E	3. E	3. C	3. D
4. A	4. D	4. E	4. E	4. D	4. A	4. A
5. C	5. C	5. A	5. C	5. B	5. E	5. E

TEST 8	TEST 9	TEST 10	TEST 11	TEST 12	TEST 13
1. E	1. A	1. E	1. C	1. B	1. B
2. D	2. D	2. B	2. C	2. C	2. D
3. E	3. E	3. E	3. D	3. D	3. B
4. E	4. E	4. C	4. C	4. B	4. A
5. B	5. E	5. E	5. C	5. A	5. C

GLOSSARY OF PURCHASING TERMS

ACKNOWLEDGMENT - A form used by a vendor to advise a purchaser that his/her order has been received. It usually implies acceptance of the order.

AS IS - A term indicating that goods offered for sale are without warranty or guarantee. The purchaser has no recourse on the seller for the quality or condition of the goods.

BID - An offer, as a price, whether for payment or acceptance. A quotation specifically given to a prospective purchaser upon his/her request, usually in competition with other vendors.

BILL OF LADING (UNIFORM) - Abbreviation: B/L or b/l. A carrier's contract and receipt for goods by which he/she agrees to transport from one place to another and to deliver to a designated person or assigns for compensation and upon such conditions as are stated therein.

> The straight bill of lading is a non-negotiable document and provides that a shipment is to be delivered direct to the party whose name is shown as consignee (buyer of the goods). The carriers do not require its surrender upon delivery except when necessary that the consignee be identified. (It's also known as the *packing slip.*)
>
> The order bill of lading is negotiable. Its surrender' endorsed by the shipper, is required by the carriers upon delivery, in accordance with the terms thereon. The object of an order bill of lading is to enable a shipper to collect for his/her shipment before it reaches destination.
>
> A clean bill of lading is one receipted by carrier for merchandise in good condition (no damage, loss, etc., apparent) and which does not bear such notations as *shipper's load and count,* etc.
>
> A foul bill of lading is one indicating that a damage or shortage existed at the time of shipment.

C. & F. (COST AND FREIGHT) - A term used when goods are to be conveyed by ocean marine transportation and meaning that the price stated includes both the cost of the goods and the transportation charges to the named point of destination.

CAVEAT EMPTOR - *Let the buyer beware* - The purchase is at the buyer's risk.

CAVEAT VENDITOR - *Let the seller beware* - The seller, in some situations, is liable to the buyer if the goods delivered are different in kind, quality, use, and purpose from those described in the contract of sale.

CENTRALIZED (TERM) CONTRACT - A contract awarded by the OGS Standards & Purchase Group for commodities which are required on a continuing basis (usually for a specified period of time).

CERTIFICATE OF COMPLIANCE - A supplier's certification to the effect that the supplies or services in question meet certain specified requirements.

C.O.D. (CASH ON DELIVERY) - Payment for purchases on delivery.

CONSIGNMENT - Goods shipped for future sale or other purpose, title remaining with the shipper (consignor), for which the receiver (consignee), upon his/her acceptance, is accountable. Consigned goods are a part of the consignor's inventory until sold. The consignee may be the eventual purchaser, may act as the agent through whom the sale is effected, or may otherwise dispose of the goods in accordance with his/her agreement with the consignor.

DISCOUNT - An allowance or deduction granted by the seller to the buyer, usually when certain stipulated conditions are met by the buyer, which reduces the cost of the goods purchased. However, discounts may be granted by the seller without reference to stipulated conditions. An example of such use of discount is the application of discount to a nominal or *list* price to establish the *net* or actual price.

An <u>arbitrary discount</u> is one agreed upon between vendor and purchaser which has no relation to the vendor's usual basis for discount.

A <u>broken package discount</u> is one applying on a quantity of goods less than the quantity contained in a vendor's regular package.

A <u>cash discount</u> is an allowance extended to encourage payment of invoice on or before a stated date which is earlier than the NET date. The percent of discount allowed is as agreed between buyer and seller and is often established by industry or trade custom. Usual discounts are 1/2, 1, and 2 percent with occasional discount allowances to 10 percent.

A <u>quantity discount</u> is an allowance determined by the quantity or value of a purchase.

ESCALATION - An amount or percent by which a contract price may be adjusted if specified contingencies occur, such as changes in the vendor's raw material or labor costs.

F.O.B. (FREE ON BOARD) - The term means the seller is required to place the goods aboard the equipment of the transporting carrier without cost to the buyer. The term *f.o.b.* must be qualified by a name of location, such as shipping point, destination; name of a city, mill, warehouse, etc. The stated f.o.b. point is usually the location where title to the goods passes from the seller to the buyer. The seller is liable for transportation charges and the risks of loss or damage to the goods up to the point where title passes to the buyer. The buyer is liable for such charges and risks after passing of title. For example, f.o.b. destination would mean that delivery costs to the destination are included. f.o.b. shipping would mean that delivery costs are <u>not</u> included.

FREIGHT AT DESTINATION - An expression meaning that freight charges will be paid by the consignee of goods upon their arrival at a specified destination.

INITIATING UNIT - The program unit that needs the commodities and/or services and prepares the Purchase Requisition.

INVITATION FOR BIDS - A request, verbal or written, which is made to prospective suppliers for their quotation on goods or services desired by the prospective purchaser.

INVOICE - A document showing the character, quantity, price, terms, nature of delivery, and other particulars of goods sold or of services rendered; a bill.

LEAD TIME - The period of time from date of ordering to the date of delivery which the buyer must reasonably allow the vendor to prepare goods for shipment.

LUMP SUM - The price agreed upon between vendor and purchaser for a group of items without breakdown of individual values; a lot price. In construction, *lump sum* means a fixed price for the complete project, as specified.

MUTUAL ASSENT - In every contract each party must agree to the same thing. Each must know what the other intends; they must mutually assent to be in agreement.

OPEN-ACCOUNT PURCHASE - A purchase made by a buyer who has established credit with the seller. Payment terms are usually stated to require payment of invoice on or before a specific date or dates; also, to require payment of invoice in full, or less a certain percentage for prompt payment. Such terms are agreed upon between buyer and seller at time of placing order, or before.

PACKING LIST or PACKING SLIP - A document which itemizes in detail the contents of a particular package or shipment (also called a straight bill of lading).

PER DIEM (Latin) - *By the day.*

PURCHASE ORDER CHANGE NOTICE - Form used by Purchase Unit to amend a previously issued Purchase Order (a price change, typographical error, vendor change, change in delivery specifications, etc.).

QUOTATION - A statement of price, terms of sale, and description of goods or services offered by a vendor to a prospective purchaser; a bid. When given in response to an inquiry, is usually considered an offer to sell. Also, the stating of the current price of a commodity; the price so stated.

REQUIREMENT LETTER - A request from the Purchasing Unit to the program units asking their anticipated needs for a commodity for a specific period of time. This data is used to prepare proposals for centralized contracts.

SERVICE CONTRACT - Contract awarded for performance of a service where the total cost is in excess of $1,000 annually.

SHIP TO ADDRESS - The program unit actually responsible for receiving merchandise and/or service against a purchase order, purchasing authorization, etc.

STANDARD VOUCHER - The document prepared by the vendor and submitted by them to secure payment for the delivered commodities and/or services.

SUBCONTRACTOR - A party who contracts with a prime contractor to perform all or any part of the prime contractor's obligations in a particular prime contract.

TERMS OF PAYMENT - All purchase transactions require a payment for the goods or services received and, excepting in an unusual exchange or barter deal, payment is made in negotiable funds in accordance with the terms agreed between buyer and seller.

WITHOUT ENGAGEMENT - A phrase incorporated in a quotation and used to avoid having to accept an order at the price quoted. A safeguard against prices fluctuating in the interval between the giving of the quotation and the order being placed.